OVERHEARD

# OVERHEARD

## david h. c. read

**ABINGDON PRESS**
Nashville New York

OVERHEARD

*Copyright © 1969, 1970, 1971 by Abingdon Press*

All rights in this book are reserved.
No part of the book may be reproduced in any manner whatsoever without written permission of the publishers except brief quotations embodied in critical articles or reviews. For information address Abingdon Press, Nashville, Tennessee.

*ISBN 0-687-29936-5*

*Library of Congress Catalog Card Number: 78-136052*

SET UP, PRINTED, AND BOUND BY THE
PARTHENON PRESS, AT NASHVILLE,
TENNESSEE, UNITED STATES OF AMERICA

To Jeremiah Milbank
*with deep affection*

# Contents

Introduction ..................................... 9

I Suppose Christianity Is on the Way Out Now ..... 11

I've Got My Own Religion:
   Who Needs a Church? ........................ 20

I Don't Know What You Mean by God ............ 30

Frankly, I'm Bored by the Bible ................... 40

About Life After Death—We Don't Know
   and I Don't Care ............................. 51

Christianity Seems So Complicated ................ 61

They're Always Talking About Sin ................ 71

I Wish Churches Would Mind
   Their Own Business ......................... 81

Religion Is for the Weak: I Don't Need a Savior .... 91

I've Tried Prayer and It Doesn't Work ............101

OVERHEARD

I'll Take Christian Ethics but Not the Fairy Tales ....111

I Suppose Christ Is Really a Kind of Myth ..........120

I Live a Pretty Decent Life:
What More Do I Need? ........................132

# INTRODUCTION

Every preacher knows that there is a huge difference between the appreciative remarks he hears from the faithful at the end of a Sunday service and the casual comments on religion that he overhears in the street, or the bus, or the doctor's waiting room. If he listens only to what he hears he might nourish the comforting illusion that most people today accept the traditional doctrines and practices of the church and are delighted to have them expounded and confirmed. If he listens to what he overhears he knows that this is a completely false picture. This is a time when few people have an unquestioning allegiance to the faith of their fathers, when thousands have kissed good-by to almost all religious beliefs and habits, and when even churchgoers are nourishing doubts about even the most fundamental dogmas of the past.

So I want to address myself to some of the remarks that one overhears. By "overhearing" I don't mean some kind of clerical eavesdropping, but tuning in as best one can to the thoughts and opinions about religion that are circulating in our world. Sometimes one literally overhears a conversation about religion, but overhearing means catching the religious mood

OVERHEARD

in secular writings—newspapers, magazines, novels, plays—and the occasional remark in a movie or a broadcast. Sometimes, too, I overhear even when a conventional remark is being made about a sermon. Behind the words there is a nagging question struggling to get out.

The remarks I have chosen for comment are, I hope, all genuine expressions of what many people are thinking and feeling about religion in America today. I have tried not to fabricate quotations to which I have a ready-made reply.

These talks were first presented on the NATIONAL RADIO PULPIT, produced by the NBC Radio in association with the Broadcasting and Film Commission of the National Council of Churches, and I am grateful they have agreed to this publication.

New York City, 1970

# I Suppose Christianity Is on the Way Out Now

Here is the kind of remark that most people hesitate to make in a preacher's presence, but which he overhears in various ways almost every week. "I suppose Christianity is on the way out now."

Some of you may have never heard anyone voice this opinion. Others may move in circles where it is accepted almost as an axiom. In between I doubt if there are many today who have never begun to wonder if Christianity has, in fact, shot its bolt. So it may be that even a loyal church member, alert to the religious drift, might be overheard saying in any unguarded moment: "I suppose Christianity is on the way out now."

If questioned, he would point to some ominous signs. He could talk about the enormous slippage in church statistics during the course of this century. In 1910 when there was an international missionary conference in Edinburgh, Scotland, most countries in Europe, including Russia, had powerful established churches, and these officially Christian countries had unrivalled power and prestige throughout the world. There was no challenging movement in sight—religious or secular—no communism, fascism, nationalism, or secularism that threatened the dominance of the Christian church. That conference could take as its motto with unbounded optimism, "The Evangelization of the World in This Generation." While there was respect at that time for the other great world religions they were not considered what in our jargon we would call "viable options." They were dead and waiting to be buried.

I hardly need to spell out the changes that two world wars, the emergence of communism, the disappearance of colonialism, and the dominance of technology have brought to the world scene. It looks as though almost everywhere the churches are on the defensive or in full retreat. Vast territories are ruled by governments that are militantly atheistic, and few nations are left with anything like an established church. Protestants, Roman Catholics, and Orthodox are all experiencing this massive onslaught of a secularized world that appears to be heading for a future in which Christianity will be a dwindling cult without influence or credibility.

Until recently the believer could reply: "Ah, yes, but things are different in the U.S.A. Here is the world's most powerful nation and never has the Christian church been stronger in numbers, in power and influence." But from what we overhear the slippage has begun here too. In a few years, according to the polls, the majority of Americans have reversed their

## I Suppose Christianity Is on the Way Out Now

opinions about the influence of the churches. In 1957, 69 percent thought that religion was increasing its influence on American life, while in 1967 the figure dropped to 23 percent—a startling change in ten years. If we ignore statistics we still are apt to draw the conclusion from what we overhear that the so-called religious boom in the U.S.A. is over. That's not enough to justify the conclusion that Christianity is on the way out, but when it's added to the total world picture it's not surprising that many are asking what the future holds.

Then there's this new mood of tolerant speculation about religion in general. The American atmosphere is not becoming antireligious, but is certainly hostile to what look like exclusive claims. "The evangelization of the world in this generation" does not only sound a hopeless proposition today, for many it sounds unnecessary or even undesirable. What I overhear is something like this: "All religions are different ways of meeting the same need. No religion that claims to be *the* way, *the* truth, and *the* life has any future in the modern world. There have been many such religions in the past that are now sunk without trace. Christianity suited a portion of this planet for some twenty centuries, but now we'll have to evolve some more comprehensive faith." Often one hears the suggestion that the new religion will have to be more "scientific"—whatever that means.

OVERHEARD

So this, roughly, is the case for the demise of Christianity—it *seems* to be happening right across the world, and, in the light of our new knowledge of comparative religion it *ought* to be happening.

Let me comment first on the evidence that Christianity is in full retreat across the world today. It may be that the situation looks desperate if we look at world statistics and the enormous forces with which today's church has to contend. But there are some things that need to be said to those who are in a hurry to write off the Christian church.

One is that this is not the first time in history when the outlook has been so bleak that observers have said "Christianity is finished." During the persecutions right at the beginning, few could have been willing to bet on the church's chances of survival. When, after the first flush of success, Christianity felt the whole weight of Roman power, Greek philosophy, and popular religion, numbers began to shrink, and in some places such as North Africa the churches were almost entirely wiped out. Then there was the period after the church's acceptance by the Emperor Constantine when the empire collapsed and Europe descended into the Dark Ages. Many at that time thought that the church was finished; the barbarians would snuff it out. In more recent times we find scholars of the eighteenth and nineteenth centuries asserting confidently that the day of Christianity was over. Voltaire writing in the 1770's reck-

I Suppose Christianity Is on the Way Out Now

oned that the Bible would be forgotten and the church a dim memory in a hundred years. We hear a lot of talk about our devout, church-going ancestors, but the evidence is the Christian church had far less hold on the population in the earlier days of this nation than it does now. Shrewd observers then must have been fairly well satisfied that its days were numbered. So the old saying is worth remembering that "the church is an anvil that has worn out many hammers."

But this reflection is not sufficient and can indeed be a snug way of refusing to face the facts. After all, false forecasts in the past don't amount to proof that the death of Christianity can never happen. So I would rather emphasize another point here that is often overlooked. It has to do with the distinction between *Christianity* as a living faith and *Christendom*, the kind of society that flourished in Europe in the Middle Ages, which lasted on practically into living memory and spread through the world as a result of the dominance of European power. The idea of Christendom was of Christian nations guided by Christian laws with an established Christian church. There are some who believe that this was a totally false idea, a radical perversion of Christianity, since it involved the church in all sorts of compromises with the state and obviously encouraged a very formal and diluted idea of what it means to be a Christian. Was there ever, in fact,

OVERHEARD

what in New Testament terms could be called a "Christian country"? I am not prepared to dismiss the ideal of Christendom as a tragic mistake. We owe too much to it. But one thing is plain. Christendom is not only on the way out, it has gone, except for the lingering idea in some countries where there is still an established church.

But is there any reason to suppose that because we can't now count all of Europe and Russia as so many million "Christians," because Anglo-Saxon missions are less powerful than in colonial days, because there are no longer any great semipolitical "princes of the church," that therefore Christianity is dying? On the contrary, it could be that now the church has shaken free from its power and prestige as an agent of a dominant culture, it may be emerging to a new and vigorous life. The modern World Council of Churches, whatever its weaknesses, is surely a more hopeful sign of Christianity's worldwide appeal than the old "missionary conference" where one particular kind of church—usually the white Anglo-Saxon—completely dominated the proceedings. What some Christians are mourning today is the decline of the influence of our own particular brand of Christianity; what others are recognizing with joy is the emergence of the World Church in which the Gospel can be revealed, stripped of the conventions and prejudices of one dominant culture. So I would dare to say that, with the demise of

## I Suppose Christianity Is on the Way Out Now

Christendom, Christianity, as a truly universal religion, may be on the threshold of a new life in which quality rather than quantity will be the criterion of vitality.

Then what do we say to those who are sure that Christianity *ought* to die because it is too narrow, too exclusive, and too much attached to one little strip of history and one particular person who lived and died two thousand years ago? What we say will depend entirely on our own estimate of that particular person. In other words, what you believe about Jesus Christ, what he means to you, will determine whether or not you can accept the thought that Christianity is bound to be on the way out. If I were an agnostic with a benevolent attitude to all reputable religions, I might decide that Christianity was due to be replaced by something new. But like everyone else who has met with the living Christ and accepted him as Lord, I cannot conceive that he can ever be superseded. It's not that I think that *my* religion is final and adequate for all time but that I have learned that *he* is. He reveals himself to me as the Lord of the future as well as the past, and the more I get to know him the surer I am that we are in no position to relegate him to the religious museum. Rather do I begin to realize that it is he who judges mankind and not mankind who decides about him.

For those who are in any way committed to the

Christian faith, there can be no question of Christ fading into the pantheon of departed gods. Rather do we feel that we have hardly begun to explore the life to which he summons us. Chesterton remarked once that the trouble with Christianity is not that it has been tried and found wanting but that it has been found difficult and not tried. When someone says: "We've had Christianity," I feel like asking if they really believe they have reached the level of life that Christ stands for and are ready for something more. And when they say: "We need something new," I want to ask: "Just what exactly? Something better than love as a way of life? An improvement on the Sermon on the Mount? A wiser, kinder God than the one we find in Christ?" Can anyone really point to a religion that offers an obviously higher way than the Christian way or a person who has clearly more to offer than Jesus Christ?

I am sure that we are going to see many new and strange developments in the religion of the future and that Christianity may be expressed in ways that are very different from the ones we know. But I am equally sure that there is no development of mankind that can make the Gospel out-of-date. It is already apparent that in the outer reaches of space the love and wisdom of God and the sustaining power of the Christian Gospel mean as much as they did by the shores of Galilee. I see no reason to

I Suppose Christianity Is on the Way Out Now

believe that humanity has outgrown the truths that Christ brings to the human mind or the strengths he imparts to the questing soul. Rather do I believe with St. Paul that "eye hath not seen, nor ear heard, neither have entered into the heart of man, the things which God hath prepared for them that love him." And I continue to believe that the surest guide into that love is the Christ who is "the same yesterday, today, and tomorrow." That is why when I overhear the opinion that Christianity is finished, I am inclined to wonder whether, on the contrary, it may not be just beginning.

# I've Got My Own Religion: Who Needs a Church?

I frequently come across the statement in books and articles by radical theologians that this is a thoroughly irreligious generation. The supernatural, they say, is out. No one believes anymore in a divine dimension. The only God who can be accepted is one who is just another name for humanity, or progress, or the evolution of the universe. Prayer, we are told, has become an impossibility for people who know what makes things tick. No one today is ready to accept anything that sounds mystical or miraculous. The average man just believes in the evidence of his senses and the omnipotence of the scientific method. It sounds as though we are the first totally secularized generation with only a few pockets of old-fashioned believers.

My own view is that this is nonsense. The evidence, as I see it, is all the other way. Seldom have men and women more eagerly been seeking for that which lies beyond the secular world with its proliferation of material goods. Surely that's part of what the youth revolt is about. It's a rejection of material values and a yearning for the transcendent.

I'VE GOT MY OWN RELIGION: WHO NEEDS A CHURCH?

There's a strongly mystical element in many of the activities that shock and surprise the older generation. The mass response to a certain musical beat, the slogans about love, the flowers and the paintings, even the use of drugs—all this is symptomatic of a mystical quest that may be profoundly religious. There is no sign whatever of a rejection of the divine or of the old rationalism that eliminated all that cannot be mathematically proved or experienced by the senses. There is more concern for the extrasensory, the transcendent than there has been at any time in living memory.

Then, again, we might ask: "If this is a skeptical and irreligious generation, how do you explain the vast popularity of horoscopes, the increasing interest in psychic phenomena and the practice of spiritism, the huge sale of charms, mascots, Ouija boards, and crystal balls, or for that matter, the flood of books on popular religion including a swelling stream on cults from the ancient or modern East? I find these signs of this generation's passionate religious quest not only in the U.S.A., but everywhere I go—in Europe, in Australia, in the Far East. On the intellectual level, books on all kinds of religion are being devoured and colleges report that schools of religion are growing on campus after campus. The other day I met a young girl of many talents, thoroughly of her generation and not from a very churchy family, and asked her what she hoped to

21

study when she went to college. "Theology," she said, as if it were the most natural thing in the world.

So, from the crudest superstition to the loftiest level of mystical devotion, the signs are that this is a most religious generation. And before I overhear the protests: "But we can't get anyone to come to the prayer meetings; my children won't go to church; the Sunday school is not what it used to be," let me make it very clear that I am *not* saying that organized religion—the life of our churches and synagogues—is flourishing. On the contrary, if I had to define in a sentence the religious mood of today I would say: "There is a yearning for the divine dimension coupled with a deep distrust and rejection of all organized religion."

This is what the preacher overhears nearly every day if his antennae are sensitive. And I've chosen a typical remark to summarize the mood. "I've got my own religion: who needs a church?" Very, very seldom is the remark made: "I don't want any religion, so you can get your church out of my hair." The rejection of the church is nearly always coupled with some expression of religious belief. The kind of thing you overhear is: "I like to do my praying on my own"; "I admire Christ but have no time for the church"; "Christianity is great, but the church is a racket"; "I can worship God much better without being jammed in a pew going through the motions"; "I don't think you can organize something spiritual";

I'VE GOT MY OWN RELIGION: WHO NEEDS A CHURCH?

"All that machinery destroys the spirit of religion"; "I can't be sincere if I accept all these creeds and rituals." What I overhear, then, is an expression of faith plus a radical dislike of all religious institutions.

I confess that there was time when I completely shared this point of view and that today I have moods when organized religion gets me down. No one, after all, is in a better position than a minister to know the stifling effect of the institution at its worst. Nearly every minister I know has sometimes a wild desire to tear up all his files and committee reports and toss them out of the window, or to stop in the middle of a service and do a somersault down the central aisle. It is this stifling feeling, more than anything else, I believe, that is leading to the number of dropouts from the ministry in so many denominations today.

Why, then, do most of us decide to stick around, and what makes the majority of committed Christians still faithful to the institution? Many suspect that it must be just habit or vested interest, but I ask any skeptic to believe that there are some solid reasons why we refuse to cut loose and nourish a private religion of our own.

Suppose we examine for a moment this notion: "I've got my own religion." Does anyone really suppose that he has thought up for himself his basic beliefs, or that they have been privately and exclusively revealed to him by God? The only people

OVERHEARD

who seem to me to be entitled to say "I've got my own religion" are those unbalanced souls who write at length to me about their private communications from God which turn out to be pathetically incomprehensible. The average man or woman who makes the remark seems cheerfully unaware that probably every item in his private creed has come to him from the community in which he was raised. And the religious expression of that community is the church. If we inquire into the concept of God, of Christian ethics, or of prayer that he holds in his "own religion," we will find that in one way or another he got them from the Christian church or it may be from the institutions of Judaism. With all their faults religious institutions have, in fact, been the carriers of the dynamic ideas and practices by which men live. In this sense the church is our mother—just as at one time our mother was for us the church. A man may see his mother's faults, may criticize her, may even—in extreme cases—cut himself off from her. But she remains his mother, the one from whom he received the gift of life. So, no matter what our view of the church may now be, she remains for most of us the mother from whom what spiritual life we have inevitably derives.

What this reveals is that religion is always communal as well as personal. Christianity, in particular, from the very beginning was a community. Jesus called his disciples one by one but immediately

I'VE GOT MY OWN RELIGION: WHO NEEDS A CHURCH?

welded them into a group, however loosely organized. Why, then, should I despise and reject the Christian group today however much I may feel it to have departed from the ideals and methods of the first community? By what logic can I detach myself from it while holding on to what seems most valuable, saying: "I've got my own religion: who needs a church?" Surely, if I believe in the Gospel that the church has preserved and proclaimed, my duty is to stay within and make my dissatisfactions felt in the reforming movement that all the great churches are experiencing today.

We may loathe organization, but the blunt fact is that for any movement to make an impact on our world some organization there has got to be. The revolt from the churches today by radical ministers, priests, and laymen who sever their connection in the name of a personal protest reminds me a little of what happened to the Edinburgh Festival of Music and the Arts. This highly organized festival spawned within a few years of its inception a rash of individual efforts in drama, poetry, and music that had nothing to do with the official program. They were private efforts on the fringe of the main events. As the years have gone by this fringe has become in itself a definitely organized body with its own organization and relationship to the festival and the city authorities. In what is being called today the "Underground Church" I see the coming together of individual rebels in just this kind of way and the inevitable emergence of just another kind of church. Get enough people together on the basis of "I've got my own religion: who needs a church?" and you'll soon have a new religious institution in our midst.

Of course, many who make this remark are not all that concerned about Christianity. I hope I am not misjudging when I say that some, at least, are using this phrase to express their desire not to be bothered with a religion that is going to make some demands on their time, their energies, or their purse. They want a religion that provides them, when necessary, with some guidance and comfort but not one that makes demands. Now it may well be that our churches often make the wrong kind of demands in the name of Christ, but at their best they remind us that Christianity is a matter of giving as well as getting. And when we seriously reflect upon what we have been given through the church surely we owe it at least some measure of support. When in the Gospels I read of the demands Christ makes upon his followers I can't help feeling that for me to slip away from the obligations of the Christian community in the name of my private religion is too easy a way out. I, for one, need the discipline of the church both to remind me of my duties and to provide an outlet for what I may have to give. The religious freelance may have the benefit of all

I'VE GOT MY OWN RELIGION: WHO NEEDS A CHURCH?

that the churches, past and present, have to offer through their thinkers, saints, artists, and charitable works, but what is he giving in return?

My friend, Dr. Lin Yutang, the Chinese philosopher and novelist, was for some forty years a self-confessed pagan and amusing critic of the churches. A few years ago he decided that the Christian view made more sense than any other and that Christ himself makes an irresistible claim on us. As soon as this happened he returned to the church and committed himself to the membership of a particular congregation. This by no means meant that he ceased to see the weaknesses and inadequacies or that he became a conventional kind of member. But he realized that his was no private religion, no matter how deeply personal, and that this is the way we can pull our weight in the Christian cause in the current world struggle. Just recently I have been reading of the spiritual pilgrimage of Malcolm Muggeridge. Here is another modern intellectual who has found his way back to a lively Christian belief, another who has found the incomparable Christ. Unlike Lin Yutang, however, he still withholds allegiance to any branch of the church—not, oddly enough, because we demand too much in the way of convictions, but because we demand too little! I would dare to forecast that he too will be driven by the logic of his convictions to identify himself with what will seem to him the least dis-

OVERHEARD

reputable of the bodies bearing the Christian name.

Yes, of course, there are all kinds of things wrong with the religious institutions we know. They can be formal, stuffy, dated, bureaucratic, smug, professional, inhuman. But I sometimes wonder if we are not sending up such a smokescreen of self-criticism from within the church today that people are being given a complete caricature of what is really going on. The next time you hear someone rip the churches to pieces, inquire gently when last he was active within one. We are so eager to advertise our weaknesses that it is not surprising that thousands are searching today in exotic religions for experiences that could be theirs within the church of their fathers. In the enormous variety and range represented by our Christian institutions, there is room for every kind of temperament in the search for a living faith that is going on today. Anyone who thinks that the churches stand for one conventional type of religious activity has never bothered to find out for himself what is being offered. It's like a man turning his back on a library of literary classics saying: "They're all the same; I don't need them any more; I've got my own ideas—and perhaps there might be something interesting in the newsstand round the corner."

If I were bold enough, then, what I should really like to say when I overhear the remark: "I've got my own religion: who needs a church?" is "You

## I'VE GOT MY OWN RELIGION: WHO NEEDS A CHURCH?

borrowed your religion, and you're paying nothing back; and you *do* need a church, because none of us can ultimately go it alone, because the church is the carrier of the faith from one generation to another, because we all need the strength and disciplines she offers—because the church needs you." I don't really put it just like that to anyone—I've too much sympathy with each individual's reasons for rejecting the church. But I am saying it now.

# I Don't Know What You Mean by God

There are some questions to which we feel like responding by saying: "If you don't ask me—I know." It's as if we instinctively know the answer but can't put it into words. And I'm not talking about abstruse and complicated concepts. (We all have trouble when we're asked to explain what we mean by "subjective and objective," "pragmatic" or "a priori.") I'm thinking of simple things like love, and truth, and beauty. You would find it very hard to explain what you mean by love, but you *know*, don't you? Try defining truth and you get into trouble, but life would be impossible if you didn't know there is such a thing. And if you are stumped when someone asks: "What do you mean by saying that picture is beautiful?" that doesn't mean you really don't know what beauty is.

If we find it hard to put into words what we mean by such fundamental values (incidentally, just what *is* a value?), it should not be surprising if you begin to stammer and mumble when someone asks: "Just what do you mean by God?" It doesn't mean that God is abstract or unreal. On the contrary, he

## I Don't Know What You Mean by God

may be to you more real and fundamental than love or truth or beauty. It looks as though the most important ingredients in our human life are the most difficult to describe. That's probably why true lovers spend a lot of time together in silence. "If you don't ask me, I know."

In recent years I seem to overhear more and more frequently this remark about religious belief: "I don't know what you mean by God." If you have ever tried to answer it you know the trouble we get into. We can try—as I'm going to try today—to give an answer, but we know the result will be unsatisfactory. It always is with things that matter most. I can explain what I mean by a typewriter much more easily than what I mean by the grace of God. But I can live without a typewriter whereas I know that I can't get through a day without the grace of God. It's the unessential things that are easiest to define.

I realize also that words are not really the best means of answering this question. If those of us who believe in God try to track down the origins of our belief, I don't think we shall find it dates to some day when you asked the old question: "Daddy, who is God?" and got some sort of muddled reply. Your parents really answered the question, not in words, but in their lives. You absorbed the fact that they didn't live carelessly and irresponsibly, but as if they were under authority. You sensed something we call "reverence" in their lives. That, I think, is how most of us come to believe in God. Jesus never tried to give a verbal answer to the question: "What do you mean by God?" In a unique way those who were near him knew the answer just by being with him. "He that hath seen me hath seen the Father," he said. So the man or woman today who really wants to know what we mean by God can best find the answer by exposing himself to the life of Christ or by catching the infection from the most genuine of his modern disciples.

However, there must be something to be *said* to the person who asks: "What do you mean by God?" There may be possibly someone listening to me who could recite the answer of the "Shorter Catechisms," but I doubt if the average man or woman today would be much enlightened if we took a deep breath and said: "God is a Spirit, infinite, eternal, and unchangeable in his being, wisdom, power, holiness, justice, goodness, and truth." That's an excellent theological statement, but it doesn't convey much meaning to the modern enquirer after God. It's too formal and abstract and, in any case, he doesn't want a secondhand answer. He wants to know what God means to me; to whom I think I'm talking when I pray; what sort of mental picture I have when I say "God." I should, therefore, respond to the question as concretely as possible in terms of our human experience. In the Gospels it is remarkable that Jesus dealt with questions in this way. He never produced a slick formula or a careful philosophical statement. He referred to some familiar experience of daily life; or he fired back another question; or he told a story.

So, when I overhear someone say: "I don't know what you mean by God," I want to explain by referring to some experiences that are common to all sensitive human beings. For instance...

I am often asked to fill up a questionnaire on behalf of someone who has applied for a job. One of the questions usually is: "Is he or she a responsible person?" That seems to mean: Is this a reliable person who can be trusted to perform allotted work faithfully and punctually? But it means something more than this. "Responsible" literally indicates that a man or woman is responding to someone or some ideal. A responsible child is responding to his parents, and, therefore, can be increasingly trusted by them. A responsible employee is responding to his boss whether he is physically present or not. But we all know that our sense of responsibility goes far beyond acknowledging the rights of parents or employers. They also are responsible, and not only to their immediate superiors. Any child of responsible parents knows that they too are under some kind of orders. And even the most powerful leader of men is responsible too—in fact, we think they ought to be peculiarly responsible. We might say

OVERHEARD

that they are responsible, as we all are, to the highest ideals we have known. But, like the majority of the human race in all ages, I prefer to think that I, and everyone else, am *personally* responsible. My ultimate responsibility is to One who brought us all into being and knows what is best for us. If I were alone on a desert island with no one to watch me, no one to make demands, no one to care what I thought or said or did, I should still be responsible to him. That, in part, is what I mean by God.

Then, I might tell how one day I came across a passage in the letters of the novelist Katherine Mansfield, who was an atheist. In it she describes waking up in her house in the south of France and being overwhelmed by the beauty of the sea, the rocks, the trees, and the flowers. Then, she added: "How I wish there were Someone to thank!" I believe that her impulse to thank Someone brought her nearer to the truth than all the arguments that had led her to deny the existence of God. I longed to have been there to say: "But, my dear, there *is* Someone to thank. There *is* One who brought it all into being, and your instinct of gratitude is the echo of his voice." Don't we all know moments when we want to shout "Thank you"—a "Thank you" that ranges far beyond any human recipient? That, in part, is what I mean by God.

Then, there is a less happy experience that, unfortunately, is equally familiar. Life is not all "thank yous"; quite often we find ourselves saying "I'm sorry." What do we mean? It may be a quite trivial expression of regret as when we bump into a stranger in the street. It may be a heartfelt confession of having offended someone we love, or an admission of having failed in some task or duty. But aren't there times when, with no human being around to reprove us or challenge our conscience, we still feel desperately sorry that we are not the sort of person we ought to be? And isn't it a very human experience to want to confess this personally to One who knows us through and through? You can't confess to an empty universe. There must be One to whom in the most basic way I can say "I'm sorry." And that, in part, is what I mean by God.

And now I would want to talk about an experience that is common, I believe, to all of us although some would be reluctant to admit to it. It has to do with the mystery of life. No matter how rationalist and matter-of-fact we may be there will be moments when we know that there is a curious dimension that eludes our mental grasp and opens up visions of rich truth beyond the evidence of our normal sense. We glimpse this as we look at a newborn baby or know a strangely transcendent sorrow as we watch the passing of one we love. It may be that at times the whole world has become transfused for us as this mysterious dimension is opened up. Only the

poets and artists can communicate this mood—
what Wordsworth called:

> That blessed mood,
> In which the burden of the mystery,
> In which the heavy and the weary weight
> Of all this unintelligible world,
> Is lightened:—that serene and blessed mood,
> In which the affections gently lead us on,—
> Until . . .
> . . . we are laid asleep
> In body, and become a living soul:
> While with an eye made quiet by the power
> Of harmony, and the deep power of joy,
> We see into the life of things.

When "we see into the life of things" we are aware, as Wordsworth was, of

> A presence that disturbs me with the joy
> Of elevated thoughts; a sense sublime
> Of something far more deeply interfused,
> Whose dwelling is the light of setting suns,
> And the round ocean, and the living air,
> And the blue sky, and in the mind of man.

It is this presence that is at least part of what I mean when I speak of God.

And, lest anyone should think that this God is only the name for a mystical experience given to

## I Don't Know What You Mean by God

poets and saints, I would tell of a group of soldiers, rugged, down-to-earth characters, who had been through the experience of years of captivity and of bombardment from the air by their own countrymen. I am thinking of the men I met in my last Stalag as a POW chaplain in World War II.

When I was transferred to their camp I found a battered, half-starved tentful of men who had been prisoners for five years and had just been marched five hundred miles across Germany from east to west, being constantly strafed by our own planes on the way. I didn't know what their reaction would be to a visit from a chaplain even though I had been a prisoner as long as they. When I got talking with them to my surprise there was one topic that came up again and again apart from the usual ones of food and liberation. It was God. They didn't talk poetically or mystically, but said things like: "I don't understand it, padre . . . I'm not a religious man, but somehow on that march there was Someone there." "Somehow there was Someone there." That, in part, is what I mean by God.

I keep saying "in part" because none of these experiences can represent all that God means to me. How could one compress into one sentence, or one story, or one poem, the meaning of the divine, the ultimate, the Lord of heaven and earth? Yet there is one point at which I would want to say: "This

OVERHEARD

is what I mean by God" in human terms without any qualification whatsoever.

I would speak of One who lived, and worked, and taught, and suffered, and was killed and came back from the dead here in the middle of our human family. I would speak of a love that was absolute and unforgettable—a life poured out for others—an infinite purity, wisdom, and compassion. I would say: "Look there at that life; listen to what he says, and you will know what he meant when he said: 'He that hath seen me hath seen the Father,' and what his apostle meant when he spoke of the glory of God reflected in the face of Christ." The more I let the qualities of Christ make their impact on my soul the more confidently I want to say: "That, my friend in human terms—which are all we have—is what I mean by God."

Perhaps, in the end, there are not so very many who can honestly say: "I don't know what you mean by God." The remark doesn't usually come from those who are outside the churches, but from those inside who have become skeptical about the God they have been taught to worship. Suddenly, the whole religious map becomes distorted and muddled for them, and they feel they have become too sophisticated to accept this God to whom we talk as son to a father. They revolt against what is called "God-talk" and claim that the word has no longer any meaning for them. In particular, they reject

## I Don't Know What You Mean by God

what they call the "illusion of a *personal* God." So let me end with a word about this.

When we say that God is "a person" we don't mean that somewhere among the billions of beings in the universe there is a bigger and better Being, a kind of superman. God cannot be a part of his own creation. "For thus saith the Lord that created the heavens . . . I am the Lord; and there is none else." Belief in a personal God means trusting in a God who has in perfection the qualities that make us persons—thought, purpose, the power of communication, and supremely, love. Such qualities are the highest that we know and so we believe in a God who can think and will and communicate and love. That is why the Bible writers were not ashamed to use the simplest language of human intercourse when talking about God, and why Jesus said we should call him "Father." The crudest forms of talking to this personal God can be, I believe, more real and true than abstract meditation on some distant abstraction.

So when I overhear the remark: "I don't know what you mean by God," perhaps the most helpful thing I could say—after all this—is just: "Try talking to him."

# Frankly, I'm Bored by the Bible

If I'm correctly tuned in to what many people of all ages are thinking today about conventional religion, one of the remarks I overhear is "Frankly, I'm bored by the Bible." Seldom will this be said out loud unless by the very young. In most sections of society no one is *supposed* to be bored with the Bible. Everyone tells us what a great book it is. Scholars speak of its magnificence as literature; politicians quote from it; commencement speakers commend it; religious people say they can't live without it; and preachers seem to find it exciting. For anyone to rise and say "I'm bored by the Bible" would be like announcing to the fans at a World Series game that baseball is a bore. You just don't say that kind of thing. If you think it you'd better keep it under your hat.

But isn't it possible that the one who makes this remark is not being blasphemous at all? He is simply being honest. If someone were to tell me that he had never in his life felt bored when reading the Bible I should have difficulty in believing him, just as I doubt the veracity of the man who says that

## FRANKLY, I'M BORED BY THE BIBLE

never in his life has he been bored in church, or bored by Shakespeare, or bored by Beethoven. There is nothing in the world so tremendous and awe-inspiring that we must always find it so. There are moments when even the greatest does not speak to us, and there are also moments when the dullness is not in what we are hearing but in our own souls. If a man is ready to admit he finds the Bible boring, we can do something about his condition. Whereas, if he goes on pretending that he is thrilled with it when, in fact, he has given up reading it he has sealed himself off from the spiritual awakening that could come his way.

I sometimes think that we in the churches have done quite a lot to make the Bible dull. Since it is, in fact, one of the most vivid and exciting collections of writings ever made, this is quite an achievement. Just think, to begin with, of the form in which the book is usually handed to us. There's the black cover with the words "Holy Bible" stamped in gold. That's hardly calculated to raise our expectations. Then, we open it and find microscopic print running down two parallel columns on each page. Then someone has numbered almost every sentence—a procedure that would wreck the most exciting novel you ever read. Add to this a sprinkling of little letters and numbers and some meaningless italics and you have a layout that suggests a reading exercise that would be as thrilling as a railroad timetable.

OVERHEARD

Then, with a kind of false reverence, we have succeeded in removing the Bible from real life as we know it. It's up there on the shelf because the idea has been nourished that it deals with a totally different world from the one we know. It's thought of as a magic volume containing either abstruse spiritual secrets or stories from a never-never-land where odd things happen such as are quite beyond our normal experience. I remember once giving a series of lectures on the content of the Bible to a group of army officers—men with a good education and the average kind of contact with the church. What many of them remarked to me was something like this: "I never knew that the Bible stories could be fitted into what we know about the history and literature of the world. I always thought that all these things were recorded about a special kind of Bible world—somehow, not quite real." No wonder there are those who find the Bible boring if we have given them the impression that it doesn't really deal with real people, real history, real problems, and the human scene we know.

Another thing we have done with the Bible is to chop it up so that we give the impression that it is either a compendium of isolated texts, or else the source of some familiar passages with a lot of uninteresting matter sandwiched in between. Of course, for practical purposes in church services we have to use short extracts, and many sermons are based on single sentences, but the result has been to discourage the reading of the Bible as we read any other book—slap through at perhaps a hundred pages per sitting. No book is going to look appetizing if it is presented as a rather stodgy pie from which we may extract a few familiar plums.

Yet, when we have made allowances for all these factors that have disguised the excitement of the Bible, there remains a more subtle reason why some find it boring. This has to do with whether or not we are vitally concerned with its subject matter. Sometimes on a bus I catch a glimpse of a book my neighbor is reading. It might have a title like *Mercantile Law in Seventeenth Century Holland*. Since my interest in that subject is less than passionate, the chances are I should find the book exceedingly dull. But the reader may well have been enthralled if that happened to be his chosen field of study. Now the Bible, on the level of great literature, has a universal human appeal, but everyone knows that its chief topic is not just men and women, but God. And there are more than a few who would say that they are not at all concerned about God. They are not sure there is such a being and profess not to care. Then the Bible talks about man's dealings with God, his demands on us, and our response to him. There's something in all of us that resists this claim and response, and a man might very well be fighting off the appeal of God when

OVERHEARD

he declares that he finds the Bible boring. If he has no desire to have his way of life disturbed by a divine voice, no real concern with such matters as forgiveness and spiritual power, then the Bible could be very dull. St. Paul once remarked that "a man who is unspiritual refuses what belongs to the Spirit of God; it is folly to him; he cannot grasp it because it needs to be judged in the light of the Spirit." That doesn't mean that there is a class of person who can never find the Bible interesting, but that so long as any of us is in an "unspiritual" state —that is, turning our backs on the question of God and the challenge of the Christian life—we will not be gripped by the message of the Scriptures.

So the first thing I would ask myself if I found the Bible boring is: "Am I really concerned about God? Do I really want to know if he has something to say to me, or am I resisting any such interference with my own way of life?" There are many who could tell us that when they came to the point of genuinely seeking God, honestly wanting to find his will, then the Bible suddenly became the most entrancing book in the world. Others would relate how they used to find the Bible boring, but once they had made a Christian decision it seemed a totally different book. I am stressing now the real purpose of the Bible—its power to bring us what we call the Word of God. It is, of course, perfectly possible for anyone sensitive to great literature and magnificent use of the English language to be thrilled by the King James Bible, whether they are serious about God or not. I have a most attractive edition of the Bible, delightful to read, called "The Bible Designed to Be Read as Literature." But the Bible is not primarily designed to be read as literature. It is designed to bring us the Word of the Living God. And when that is what we really want, its pages spring to life.

Once we have faced this primary question: Do I seriously want to hear who God is and what he wants with mankind, and with me?—then we can deal with the other obstacles in our way.

It is not beyond the resources of anyone in our society today to equip themselves with a readable edition. Not only can we buy the King James or the Revised Standard in readable print and modern layout, but we can get paperback editions of the New Testament in the New English Bible edition, or the charming *Good News for Modern Man,* or the translation by J. B. Phillips. Since these are having enormous sales at the moment and are not designed to be elegant ornaments of the coffee table, we must believe that thousands are, in fact, discovering what a fascinating book the Bible is. I've met men and women who have been delighted by the discovery that one can read a whole Gospel easily in one sitting, and even begin to understand what St. Paul was talking about just by getting hold of one of these modern versions of the New Testament. Many are discovering the excitement of finding out what Jesus really said and did and what the writers believed about him, perhaps for the first time.

It then becomes not too difficult to cope with the apparently stodgy portions of the Scriptures. We will realize that it doesn't necessarily make sense to decide to read the Bible right through in exactly the order we find it. How many eager souls have begun like this, found the Genesis narratives fascinating, the story of Exodus enthralling, only to come to a slow stop somewhere in the middle of Leviticus among the minute details of the Hebrew laws. These ritual laws, the more obscure parts of the prophets, even the genealogies, have their place in the total pictures the Bible brings us, but they are not of vital importance to all people at all times. The Bible was written over a long stretch of time and speaks in all its parts to some people at some particular time. It doesn't follow that all its contents are going to be the Word of God for me right now. I wouldn't want to scrap any portion of Scripture (I remember a German friend telling me how the Book of Revelation had always seemed to him a useless and incomprehensible book until during the war he was imprisoned by the Gestapo and suddenly that book became astonishingly alive), but I suggest that we use common sense in choosing the sections with which to begin a serious reading of the Bible.

My next suggestion would be to situate the Bible

in real human life and not to treat it as a kind of mystery that requires some key to unlock. Lots of people will offer you their special theory about the Bible and imply that you can't understand it unless you accept this key. Approach it with an open mind and heart and let the Bible speak for itself. You will soon enough find out that it has a different flavor from other books, that there is a spiritual quality about it which explains why it has been called the "Word of God." But you don't need to figure out beforehand what this "Word of God" must mean. You will soon discover why it has been called "inspired," but you don't need anyone to impose on you *their* view of the nature of its inspiration. Let it speak in all the vast variety of its history, homily, poetry, and drama, in all the different accents of its human writers. Find out more about the circumstances in which each book was composed; use the new resources that are available for understanding; get hold of good commentaries to give you background and explanation if you will—but, above all, just let these books speak for themselves. And the witness of over two thousand years guarantees that you will not be bored!

It occurs to me that those who find the Bible boring are those for whom the whole field of religion seems arid and dull. They have decided that taking God seriously is going to mean accepting a restricted, cramped style of life. The Bible is just part of a whole religious pattern that blankets all the joy and exuberance of life. Its black covers are for them symbolic of a gloomy outlook that negates the zest and excitement of the natural man. Well, there may have been times when the devout gave this impression, and there may be people today who live on the assumption that God is a killjoy and, therefore, anything enjoyable is probably wrong.

My answer to them would be that exactly the opposite is true. The facts reveal that it is usually the men and women who have accepted the disciplines of religion, for whom the will of God is real, who are the ones who know what real liberty and gaiety of spirit can be. We have surely by now seen through the proposition that the abandonment of any controls or disciplines leads to a joyful freedom and lightheartedness. At the moment we are living through a period of almost complete license in what can be printed or presented on a stage. And would anyone claim that the modern novel or the modern theater is scintillating with joy and reflecting a happy liberation of the human spirit? Is it not very obvious that the obliteration of standards and the rejection of any religious restraint is producing some of the most boring and depressing material we have ever seen? Pornography ad nauseam is just that, ad nauseam; it leads to the nausea of the most utter boredom. And what can be more boring than the cult of nudity when there is nothing left to reveal?

FRANKLY, I'M BORED BY THE BIBLE

I am not pleading for any kind of primness and priggery that is afraid to call a spade a spade. The Bible certainly isn't. Its writers were much less afraid of realistic writing than most religious authors today. The point is that behind all their words lies the summons to accept the will of God; and they reveal to us that it is within this will, and not in rebellion against it, that man finds his true freedom and greatest enjoyment. Does anyone suppose that the Emperor Tiberius was a happier man than Francis of Assisi or that Don Juan, the libertine, knew more real ecstasy than John Donne, the Christian poet? The Bible is crammed with the excitement of men who have glimpsed the glory of God and, therefore, have reveled in the beauties of his creation and the variety of human experience. "The heavens declare the glory of God and the firmament showeth his handiwork." "Thou shalt rejoice in every good thing which the Lord thy God hath given unto thee." This is the freedom, the enjoyment, the celebration that rises from the accepting and believing spirit. It is those who are meek enough, humble enough, to seek the will of God who, according to Christ, inherit the earth. Even when the Bible is concerned with the other side of this picture, with life lived in defiance of the will of God, no one could call it boring. For some of the most moving stories, some of the most exciting histories are those in which the Bible writers describe the adventures

OVERHEARD

and the catastrophes of mankind astray from God.

So when I overhear the remark that the Bible is a bore, I suspect that the speaker is clinging to this old notion that religion is dull and irreligion exciting, and I long for them to make the discovery that the opposite is true. Hell, the symbol of a godless life, is infinitely boring. Heaven, contrary to popular mythology, is surely the state of the utmost excitement and enjoyment. The latest pornographic bestseller will probably be infinitely more boring than what to you are the dullest passages in the Bible. We need to take the blinkers off and recognize that a book which is concerned with our communion with God and with our neighbors is the most important, the most exciting, the most life-expanding book that can ever come our way.

# About Life After Death—
# We Don't Know and
# I Don't Care

I can imagine someone wanting to say: "About the last thing you're likely to overhear today is a conversation about life after death. Most people are far too occupied with problems on earth to worry about heaven, and in any case death is a taboo subject in modern America."

Well, I'm not so sure. Certainly this is not a subject you casually bring up at the dinner table, and as a generation we are not given to chatting about eternity. The question of life after death seems to belong, rather, to the intimate moments at a time of bereavement rather than to those snatches of conversation that one overhears. Yet it takes only a newspaper account of a medium's claim to be in contact with the dead or some prominent cleric's denial of the Christian doctrine of eternal life to set tongues wagging in all kinds of unlikely places. And it's the remark that I overhear at such a time that I'm talking about—not the groping for an answer in a moment of anguish. When people get to this topic in a de-

OVERHEARD

tached, argumentative way, someone is almost sure to say by way of disposing of the subject once and for all: "We don't know, and I don't care." What he means is that we are wasting our time even considering the question of life after death because no one has any real knowledge about it, and no modest, unassuming person should even want to live forever. That seems to settle the argument and leave nothing else to be said. No one usually can produce what looks like scientific proof of immortality, nor does anyone want to seem arrogant enough to claim it as his right. So the sensible, no-nonsense, modern attitude must surely be: "We don't know—there's no compelling evidence for survival, and I don't care—this life is enough for me."

This remark *sounds* conclusive, but is it? Let's take the second half and think about it for a while. "I don't care." If I were to butt into the conversation at this point I would want to ask respectfully if this is really true. It seems a manly, stoical, and decently humble attitude to take, especially when we contrast it with the groveling anxiety that religious people sometimes reveal or the self-centered arrogance of a hymn like "When the roll is called up yonder *I'll* be there." But the question of eternal life is not just a selfish question. Surely it concerns the destiny of those we love. It's all very well for a man to say he doesn't care about his own destiny,

## ABOUT LIFE AFTER DEATH

but how many honestly don't care about others? I have heard this remark in a student bull session, but never from a man or woman who has just suffered a bereavement. There's nothing noble about the "I don't care" attitude when it applies to those we deeply love, and I doubt whether anyone really feels that way at such a time. We do care and care immensely, whether or not this is the end.

There is a moving story in the Old Testament about King David mourning the loss of his infant child. When the news was gently broken to him he surprised his friends by stopping his fast and resuming his normal life. And this is how he voiced the reasoning of his anguish: "While the child was yet alive, I fasted and wept; for I said, 'Who knows whether the Lord will be gracious to me, that the child may live?' But now he is dead; why should I fast? Can I bring him back again? I shall go to him, but he will not return to me." Here is a noble— a stoic acceptance, if you will, but it is very far from the callous "I don't care." Of course he cared. And, in the light of all that he had learned about God he summed up his confidence in the words "I shall go to him." Whether it is a man of David's time, or Martha in the New Testament at the grave of her brother Lazarus, or the last family I have seen in my parish today in their hour of sorrow, never, never, do we hear the words "I don't care." The great classics of literature in every language are filled with evidence that, whether or not men have found the answers, they care intensely about the fate of those they love.

And is it even true for a man's own self that he doesn't care? Who can read another's inmost mind? Perhaps there are some around us who have genuinely brought themselves to the point of being indifferent about what happens to them after death. But I don't take too much account of what a man or woman says at a time of youth, and health, and prosperity. We don't really know whether we care or not until the shadows come down or until we face the prospect of immediate death in war or accident. I doubt very much if there are any at such moments who are completely indifferent to the question about what comes next. Perhaps those who have been conditioned by an atheist society can die without a flicker of interest in immortality, but I wonder. Certainly anyone who has been exposed to any kind of religious conviction is bound to ask the ultimate question, even if it is only in the groping mood of Hamlet:

> To die, to sleep;
> To sleep: perchance to dream: ay, there's the rub;
> For in that sleep of death what dreams may come,
> When we have shuffled off this mortal coil,
> Must give us pause.

## About Life After Death

It seems to me that unless one is totally persuaded that death is the end any normal human being is bound to think about the possibilities of a life beyond. And when we contemplate what these possibilities might be compared to our brief span here on earth, does it really make sense to say we do not care? Is there really anything noble in saying we do not care whether or not there will be a chance to develop these insights that have come to us in our best moments, whether or not we may be able to go on towards these moral goals we have hardly begun to reach, whether or not there is some dimension in which the whole tattered history of mankind will find fulfillment? Can any sensible person say he doesn't care whether this mystery we call the "self" can voyage farther into the unknown or is snuffed out when we cease to breathe?

The more I think about it the clearer it becomes that those who say "I don't care" have really already convinced themselves that there is no possibility of any such farther, richer life. So now we must examine the phrase "We don't know." Often what is meant by it is, in fact, "We do know—we know that there is nothing whatever beyond the grave."

But let's take the statement at its face value 'We don't know." My first comment would be: Right! We don't *know*—if by "know" you mean having exact, scientific information about conditions beyond the grave. The only ones to claim that we have such

## Overheard

information are those who have been persuaded by the evidence of psychic research or their experience with mediums. But the general consensus of the scientific world would be that this kind of evidence is not yet acceptable as proof of immortality. If it were, then every rational person would have to believe, and that is clearly not the case. At the same time, it should be noted that there is no possible scientific evidence that would refute such convictions. It seems to me that the correct scientific attitude is agnostic: "We don't know."

Then I would go on to observe that there is another kind of knowledge by which we live. In fact, very little of our life is ordered by strictly probable scientific facts. We "know" that Shakespeare is a better poet than Aunt Jane, but we can't prove it. We know that we love our parents, but we can't prove it. We know that to be unselfish is better than to be greedy, but we can't prove it. This kind of knowledge is even more important than the strictly scientific, and it comes to us in a different way. Call it instinctive, intuitive, extrasensory, or whatever you like, it is borne in on us by our experience to which we respond in faith. So the church has no qualms about saying that its teaching about eternal life is a matter of faith. Of course it is. Anything outside the range of our immediate observation is a matter of faith. The man who denies eternal life does so by faith quite as much as the man who

## About Life After Death

believes in it. We reach such knowledge by our response to such light as has been given us.

I know there are some Christians who would want to maintain that the resurrection of Christ offers clear proof of life beyond the grave. To me it does, but only because, for other reasons, I have accepted him as my Lord. I have faith in him, and therefore I am persuaded of eternal life since he rose from the dead. It's not that I was first convinced by the evidence for the Resurrection, then came to believe in him. As a matter of record, the majority of the contemporaries were not convinced by that evidence. Otherwise everyone within range of that event would have automatically become Christian. It is faith in Christ that gives the knowledge of eternal life, not the other way round. And faith, as the writer to the Hebrews put it, ". . . is the substance of things hoped for, the evidence of things not seen." That doesn't mean that our conviction is any less solid. It was such faith that has inspired the greatest lives in all human history, the men and women who have been able to say: "I am persuaded that neither death nor life . . . can separate us from the love of God which is in Christ Jesus our Lord."

When you come to think of it we can never have exact, scientific knowledge of anything in the future. We can talk about statistical probabilities, inevitable consequences and the like, but there is always an element of doubt. The odds against the sun failing

OVERHEARD

to rise tomorrow morning are enormous, but we still don't *know*, an unexpected cosmic collision might destroy our solar system overnight. It is *almost* certain that man will continue his space explorations, but not quite. We *assume* that we shall have enough to eat next year, but we can't prove it. Yet, this theoretical uncertainty doesn't stop any normal human being from planning ahead; otherwise life would be impossible.

Most of us from time to time peer into our own future and wonder what is coming. As children we wonder what it will be like to be grown-up. When we go through the door of adolescence we begin to think of that other room ahead of us when we shall have made some kind of imprint through job and family. Then the next stage comes and the room ahead is perhaps labeled "retirement," and millions are planning for the time they reach it. Of course, we don't *know* at any stage whether or not we shall ever get to the next room or what it will be like if we do. We plan and act in faith. We can hardly imagine anyone saying about any part of the life ahead of them: "We don't know, and I don't care." We care tremendously, and we plan ahead in faith guided by such light as is given us.

Surely then we shall do the same when we contemplate that mysterious room we enter when this mortal life is over. We do not know what it will be like. We have even less chance of guessing this time since our environment will have completely changed. If someone says "There . . . is no such room; you just come to a full stop," we can only say "How do you know?" You can't decide such a question by counting heads; but if I were tempted to believe that death is the end I would be arrested by the fact that the vast majority of the men and women I admire the most lived and died in the conviction that it is not. Among them, of course, is Christ himself. If we profess confidence in him as our Lord and God, the question is surely settled. But even if we just accept him as the supreme teacher about God and man, is it possible that he would lead us astray in this momentous matter? Listen to these solemn and simple words: "In my Father's house are many rooms; if it were not so, would I have told you that I go to prepare a place for you?" I find these words more powerful than any philosophic argument for immortality. "Rooms"—yes, for him there is a room beyond death and more than one.

This is the view of life that comes when God is real. Without him we should have to say "We don't know, but it looks like a dead end." With him life becomes open-ended, and there shines from those rooms ahead a resurrection light. The New Testament tells us everywhere that we can begin to live now with this kind of knowledge. ". . . this is life eternal, that they may know thee the only true

OVERHEARD

God, and Jesus Christ, whom thou hast sent." When we know this God we are already in touch with One who is not bounded by our mortal vision or subject to the frailties of our flesh. And the more nearly we know him the more our confidence in that unimaginable future grows. ". . . as it is written, eye hath not seen, nor ear heard, neither have entered into the heart of man, the things which God hath prepared for them that love him."

So, instead of saying: "We don't know, and I don't care," the Christian sets his faith in the God he has come to know and love, and cares very much that his life is on the track that leads to the ultimate communion with God with all the saints. We realize that there is much in us that is not worthy of eternity, but we have our glimpses of the kind of life that comes to fulfillment in those rooms beyond. Without any pretense of having private information about conditions beyond the grave, we can say that in our best moments we have the clues that faith can follow, "while we look not at the things which are seen, but at the things which are not seen: for the things which are seen are temporal; but the things which are not seen are eternal."

# Christianity Seems So Complicated

"Christianity seems so complicated." Yes; I know what you mean. Who knows it better than one who has spent years with the theologians, who is constantly trying to answer questions about the faith, who is immersed in the machinery of the church, and who is daily exposed to the vast network of ideas, programs, dialogs, reports, and social activities that make up modern Christianity. Many a minister finds himself wondering at times if there isn't a simpler way of expressing the Gospel that Christ brought into the world.

And yet what keeps me and others in the ministry is an elemental simplicity at the heart of it all. The Christianity I know and believe in is not dependent on the mastery of great systems of theology, nor is it expressed chiefly by the ramifications of church life in this complicated age. One of the most learned theologians I have ever known, John Baillie, expressed the heart of his faith in a little book of private prayers that anyone can understand and use. And sometimes when I find myself standing before a big congregation in the center of the city with a little child in my arms and saying: "See what love the Father has given us, that we should be called the children of God," then all the complications and the machinery of church life seem to drop away, and we are just near to God.

Still, I can understand that we must seem at times to offer an abstruse and baffling set of propositions for men and women to believe in and to wrap them up in a very complicated institution. It was Cardinal Cushing who as a young priest found himself asking the victim of an accident: 'Do you believe in one God in three persons—Father, Son and Holy Spirit," and received the answer: "Here I am dying, and you're asking me riddles." And it must be hard for a serious inquirer to penetrate the jungle of our rituals and formalities to arrive at the heart of the Gospel. Sometimes the noise of ecclesiastical wheels going round is so deafening that it drowns the voice of One who is saying follow me. I like to think of Albert Schweitzer who knew the convolutions of Christian doctrine and in particular the myriad different interpretations of the life of Christ better than almost any contemporary finishing his huge volume *The Quest of the Historical Jesus* with these words:

He comes to us as One unknown, without a name, as of old, by the lake side, He came to those men who knew Him not. He speaks to us the same word: "Follow thou

## CHRISTIANITY SEEMS SO COMPLICATED

me!" and sets us to the tasks which He has to fulfill for our time. He commands. And to those who obey Him, whether they be wise or simple, He will reveal Himself in the toils, the conflicts, the suffering which they shall pass through in His fellowship, and, as an ineffable mystery, they shall learn in their own experience Who He is.

That doesn't sound so terribly complicated, does it?

At the same time I don't want to leave the impression that there is nothing complicated about Christianity. I am suspicious of anyone who tries to oversimplify and tells us to forget all about the great doctrines of the faith and that we'd all get along much better if we scrapped all the institutions of the church. The plain fact is that life is complicated, and there must be some complications about a religion that is designed to relate to every part of it. On the crudest physical level keeping alive is, after all, very simple. We just breathe and eat and sleep. But the moment we examine the structure of the human body and the processes that are involved in these actions, we are astounded at the immensely complicated machinery we carry around. You and I don't need to understand much about what is going on in these bodies of ours, but when something goes wrong we are glad that someone does. Similarly, while we can lead a Christian life without much understanding of theology, it is good that some are devoting themselves to the complications of the faith.

Again, any one of us is capable of retiring to a quiet spot and living simply with nature like Thoreau, whose motto was "Simplify, simplify." But the vast majority have to learn to live in the intricate network of a modern town or city. In the same way I can withdraw to a cell and devote myself to prayer, but most Christians have to relate their faith to the complicated traffic of our technical society.

So it would be dishonest of me to claim that we can ignore the complications and find the whole truth in some simple proposition. Those who have offered such simplifications have often led people astray, either because their simplification was a distortion or was inadequate or was perhaps not as simple as they thought. I am thinking, for instance, of those who say: "Join my sect: We've got all the truth; just go along with us and you needn't worry about thinking through all the problems of religion." That could be very simple, but it would be a distortion of the Gospel with its appeal for personal conviction and being able to give a reason for the faith that is in us. I am thinking again of those who say: "Forget all about these creeds and confessions. Christianity just means loving God and your neighbor." How often have I overheard some-

## CHRISTIANITY SEEMS SO COMPLICATED

thing like that! What is claimed to be essential Christianity is very important, but it cannot be the Gospel—for it contains nothing uniquely Christian. This commandment we got from Judaism. It is the first commandment of all according to Christ, but it cannot express all that he came to say, to do, and to die for. Then I am thinking of others who talk much about the "simple Gospel," but when we hear it we find ourselves confronted with an exceedingly complicated doctrine of the Atonement. No, there are no shortcuts. At heart there is a simple power, a simple attitude, a simple obedience. But its working out will always involve us in hard thought and complicated action.

If someone asks: "How can something be complicated and simple at the same time?" I would tell of a parallel experience with which we are all familiar. Let me speak of what is known as patriotism or love of country. In spite of all our divisions in the land today and the suspicions that the word "patriotism" conjures up in some minds, surely this is a genuine element in everyone's experience. We may differ enormously in our interpretation of patriotism, but it is a universal human trait to love the country of one's birth or adoption. Now, at heart, this is a very simple matter—so simple we normally don't think much about it at all. Anyone can be a true patriot whatever his I.Q., social position, color, or abilities. We love our country—that's all.

OVERHEARD

So there's nothing complicated about that. But the moment we start thinking about the implications of true love of country what a huge vista opens out. Intellectually we have to interpret our patriotism by deciding which forms of government should be supported as best for the country, which leaders should be chosen, what policies are best, how freedom can be related to order, how our patriotism can be harmonized with the patriotism of other peoples in the cause of world peace, and a host of other similar problems. Practically, our love of country involves us in a great network of obligations ranging from voting in elections to paying our taxes. Probably no two people would completely agree in their expression of patriotism. One may be very conscious of the history of the United States; another may be chiefly concerned with the future; another may feel a great emotional tug when the symbols of the nation are displayed; another may be quite unemotional and express his patriotism in working for improved conditions and social justice. When we think of great national leaders, Washington, Jefferson, Lincoln, or the men and women of our own day who have left their stamp on the nation, we will be struck by their diversity of character and temperament. There have been statesmen of opposed political parties, legislators, executives, soldiers, idealists, crusaders for different causes, inventors, scientists, artists—all of

## CHRISTIANITY SEEMS SO COMPLICATED

whom loved their country and expressed that love in their own way.

It should not be difficult, then, to see how Christianity can be both simple in its roots and yet enormously complicated in its expression. From the moment Jesus beckoned to an odd variety of men and said "Follow me," there has been an expansion of the implications of discipleship as the church moved out into all the world. The initial decision to follow Christ is not at all complicated. Millions have made it at an early age before the complexities of life have caught up with them. And at any moment, even in the midst of the confusions of our intricate society, a man or woman can catch the vision of Christ and say "That's the way I want to go." But, young or old, we shall then discover that the faith to which we are committed opens out into continuous new horizons of thought and action. If it doesn't, then we are keeping our faith in an isolation booth with no contact with the real world, and we shall earn the condemnation of the man who took his talent and hid it in the ground.

When someone says "Christianity is so complicated," I would want to say "No; not complicated, but comprehensive." That's the better word. "Complicated" suggests unnecessary elaboration. We've all known people who can take a simple subject and wrap it up in so much verbiage that we lose all interest, or others who never take the obvious route

OVERHEARD

to solving a problem but love to be devious and obscure. Christians have been guilty of doing that with their faith, but the truth is that Christianity is comprehensive rather than complicated in this sense. That is to say, it covers the whole of human life and thought. There is a richness in the faith that can satisfy the most inquiring mind and a breadth in its application that makes room for every temperament and talent. We may rightly lament the complications caused by the division of the church into rival denominations and should be praying and working for the restoration of her unity. We should rejoice in all the signs of increased understanding and cooperation in recent years. But the best ecumenical leaders know very well that the one church we believe in must never be a monolithic organization with total uniformity of worship and belief. I have no desire to warm over the complicated arguments that split the church in the past, but I believe in a comprehensive church that has room for a great variety of expressions of the faith in creed, worship, and social action.

"Come unto me," says Christ, the simplest invitation ever given to men in the history of religion. Yet, when we stop to think about these simple words what depths we begin to sound! Can anyone speak like that who is a mere man among others? Then who is he? How is he related to the God we must love and serve? What is this spiritual authority he

## Christianity Seems So Complicated

has that makes a man or woman respond to such an invitation? And what is this faith that moves us to respond? What difference does our coming to him make in our daily life? No wonder he followed up this invitation by saying "and learn of me." There is so much to learn. Nothing could be simpler than the first response, but if we stop there we shall miss the wonder and the mystery, the satisfaction and the strengthening that come with our exploration and mastery of the doctrines of Christ and their application to our life today. Christianity is not something that we grab in a moment of emotion and then carry on as before. Neither is it a kind of ticket for heaven to be accepted and then pocketed for future reference. After the invitation comes the education. Our simple act of faith is the doorway into a comprehensive religion that spans the universe in its thinking and finds practical expression in a million different ways.

Its simplicity lies in one word—love. The Fourth Gospel tells us that the Risen Christ had one question for the disciple who had denied him but was destined to be a great leader of the church. "Simon, son of Jonas, lovest thou me?" Three times the question came, just as three times Peter had denied his Lord. "Lovest thou me?" That is what matters. In spite of our confusion with this word "love" today— it can mean anything from lust to self-sacrifice— we have all a fair idea of what it means on Jesus' lips. The heart of Christianity is our love for Christ, our loyalty to him, our desire to enthrone him at the center where Self is apt to reign. There is nothing complicated about making Peter's reply: "Yea, Lord, thou knowest that I love thee." And if, for a moment we imagine that a mere feeling is enough, we have his equally simple words: "If ye love me, keep my commandments." And that is where the complications, the right, true, good, and necessary complications, set in. But through them all there shines this Light, the Christ whom we love and through whom there flows to us the guiding and strengthening grace of God.

My study shelves are loaded with books, ancient and modern, in which men and women have wrestled with the doctrines and practices of Christianity. And I have copies of dozens of creeds and catechisms in which every part of the church has tried to express the essence of the faith. Among those I have found helpful in recent years are the Presbyterian Confession of 1967 and the "New Catechism" of the Dutch Catholics. But often I find myself turning back to an old document known as the "Heidelberg Catechism" to read again the first question and hear again its answer. Let me close with these simple and moving words: "What is your only comfort, in life and in death?" "That I belong—body and soul, in life and in death—not to myself but to my faithful Savior, Jesus Christ."

# They're Always Talking About Sin

Among the reasons given for staying away from the churches today is the complaint "They're always talking about sin." You can overhear this remark wherever two or three are gathered together to voice their objections to preachers or conventional religion. Sometimes this judgment may be the result of personal experience in a church where little else was talked about from the pulpit, and where other people's sins were the chief preoccupation of the congregation. The experience may date back about fifty years, but the complainer doesn't bother to check in and see if it's still true about the church round the corner. More often, I suspect, those who say this have very little experience with the Christian church and just go on repeating the accusation. For any stigma, as Chesterton used to say, will do to beat a dogma.

So deeply is the idea rooted that we're always talking about sin, some people seem to hear us talking about sin when we haven't even mentioned the word. Not long ago when I had hardly used the

OVERHEARD

word at all in a series of radio talks I received a letter from a listener protesting against my harping on the subject of sin. It's almost as though a certain kind of person listens to a sermon with his guard up against an attack he is sure is going to be launched against him.

> There was a young lady of Surrey,
> Who departed from church in a flurry.
> Though he didn't say *sin*
> He got under my skin,
> And I'm worried I'm starting to worry.

What strikes me, however, is not the frequency but the scarcity of references to sin in the modern pulpit. In the major denominations for many years now there has been an obvious reluctance to talk about it at all. If you read through the sermon topics advertised in a big city newspaper, it is very rarely that you will ever see the word "sin." Far from *always* talking about it we seem to be *never* talking about it. In New York City you are far more likely to find the word "sin" on a movie marquee or a lurid paperback cover than a church notice board. It's as though the churches had handed the word over to be exploited by the modern merchants of sensation and sex.

I can understand the person who says he doesn't want to go to church to have his nose rubbed in the seamy side of life, and I can understand the swing

## They're Always Talking About Sin

away from the denunciatory style of preaching. After all, it is a Gospel we have to preach, and "gospel" means good news. There's little enough good news around today either in the daily paper or popular literature, so surely the churches don't need to underline the fact that there's something wrong with the human race. The secular world, in effect, is doing that for us. Sin is more effectively displayed—or at least the results of it—by the mass media than by the most eloquent sermon.

With all this in mind let me now try to explain why I believe that the church must continue to talk about sin while announcing the good news. What people probably have in mind when they complain about it is the impression we give that we disapprove of too many things that the average man considers harmless or even enjoyable. The complaint is not about our talking of sin, so much as sins. In other words, we are not explaining the biblical doctrine of sin, but are constantly labeling and judging certain habits and practices as sinful. So a great many people of honesty and goodwill are reluctant to associate themselves with a community that seems to impose a lot of moral rules with which they cannot agree. They recognize that a church has a duty to maintain Christian standards but they are worried about the priorities. So often we seem to concentrate on minor matters while saying little or nothing about the great evils that tear our society apart. As Jesus said: "You strain off a midge, yet gulp down a camel!" I believe that things will come into focus if we understand better in the first place what the church means by *sin* as something that affects us all, a fundamental condition of the human race.

When the English philosopher, C. E. M. Joad, after years as a fairly militant agnostic announced his conversion to the Christian faith shortly after World War II, he said that what had convinced him was primarily the Church's doctrine of original sin. That puzzled and shocked a lot of people, but what he was saying was simply that the biblical analysis of what is wrong with mankind seemed to him in the end to make more sense than any other. Unfortunately, as soon as you say "original sin" lots of people think you are talking about some theory of the physical inheritance by each generation, of some taint derived from the transgression of a distant ancestor called Adam. Adam means "man" and what the Genesis story is telling us is about what is fundamentally wrong with the human race and what is wrong with us now. Original sin refers to the flaw in human nature that gives us all a bias towards evil—the sort of evil that could be described as the root selfishness that cuts us off from God and our fellow men. The Bible shows very clearly that there is something wrong with the human race, that none of us is the innocent, totally well-disposed creature we often think we are.

## They're Always Talking About Sin

It used to be fashionable to dismiss this view of humanity as hopelessly pessimistic. The popular theory was that there is nothing wrong with the human race that a little more education and psychological tinkering could not put right. Now the pendulum has swung in the other direction, and we keep hearing the most despairing estimates of humanity. "What's got into people?" "How can they be so brutal, so selfish, so cruel, so indifferent to the suffering of others?" That's what we hear; and our novelists and playwrights delight to picture us as monsters of corruption. There is no one so bitter and cynical as the disillusioned idealist. If you once believed that humanity is in good shape, fundamentally sound and with no need of divine help to achieve a perfect society, then present conditions might well turn you into a cynic. But if you had really absorbed the biblical doctrine of sin such disillusionment would never happen. You would have been armed against false expectations, and ready even now to believe that the position is not hopeless.

The Fourth Gospel tells us of Christ that "he knew what was in man." And quite clearly what he knew was not only the good and the happy. It is often said, with truth, that he had infinite confidence in man's possibilities, that he saw every single man and woman as a potential son and daughter of God. But the evidence is clear that his confidence was in the grace of God, and his image reflected in the human heart and not in the intrinsic goodness of humanity. "Out of the heart," he said on one occasion, "proceed evil thoughts, murders, adulteries, fornications, thefts, false witness, blasphemies." That's a pretty tough diagnosis of what we're like inside.

I said "we" for Christ is talking about the sin in all of us. Too often the church has talked as if the sinners were the people outside while we are good religious people. There is no trace in his words or actions of this division of the world into good guys and bad guys, the righteous and the unrighteous. Time and again the thrust of his teaching is to show how bad what we call "nice" people are, and how potentially good the not-nice. This is where the Gospels turn upside down the tepid morality that often prevails in our churches. When he is talking about man's basic badness he is talking about everybody—the respectable and devout every bit as much as the outcasts of society. He had no use for a classification of sins whereby the more spectacular sins of the flesh rate higher than what we call "mere" jealousy, lovelessness, or malignant thought and talk. He "knew what was in man," and how thin the line can be between our respectable behavior and the primitive passions that lurk below.

We don't have to keep harping on the subject of our sin, but how can we understand what Christ came to do unless we realize our desperate need?

## They're Always Talking About Sin

He said that he "came to seek and to save that which was lost." If we don't feel our lostness, our lost communion with God and our fellow man, then how can we recognize the One who came to find us and restore that communion? Membership in the church signifies for most of us acceptance of Christ as "Lord and Savior." If there is nothing fundamentally wrong with us, why should we need a Savior? Anyone who reads the New Testament carefully will discover that Christ saw in mankind an evil so basic that there was no way to overcome it save by the total sacrifice of his life, the yielding of his body and soul to this sinful humanity that culminated at Calvary. If man is naturally "nice" then no Cross need ever have risen to receive the Son of God. It is there we begin to learn what sin really is.

What I have been trying to say is that if we are indeed talking about sin in the churches, it should never be just a bewailing of human faults and weaknesses, still less an attack on the frailties of those outside our fellowship. It should be a simple recognition that there is something fundamentally wrong with us, all of us, that only the grace of God can put right. Jesus once remarked with delicate irony that "people who are well do not need a doctor, but only those who are sick." No one was too sick for him to cure. The only ones he could do nothing with were those who thought they were perfectly well.

Now I want to turn to the other side of the story

of what Christ saw in men. Just as he would not have come to give himself for men if there were nothing seriously wrong, so he would not have come if he didn't believe we were worth redeeming. Just as the Christian diagnosis of sin is so radical, so is the Christian Gospel. It proclaims that every one of us is potentially a son or daughter of God—which means nothing less than growth into the image of Christ both here and hereafter. If the Christian is more aware than the skeptic of the demonic depths of human evil, he is surely also much more aware of his angelic potential. At this point in our history I feel that it is this note of hope, of expectation, of celebration that should be sounding in the churches much more than the dismal analyses of our sins. After all, we don't think of a doctor simply as the one who tells us what is wrong with us but as the one from whom we have real hopes of healing.

Most churches have somewhere at the beginning of their Sunday worship a prayer known as "Confession of Sin," followed by an absolution or declaration of pardon. Like other elements in worship these can often flow over our heads as familiar sounds without meaning. I sometimes have a daydream in which, after a congregation has murmured the words of confession and I have declared the assurance that we are forgiven, I interrupt the service by calling out: "Hi there, you! Did anything happen?" For a minister, too, it is only too easy to repeat the fa-

## They're Always Talking About Sin

miliar promises of the Gospel without realizing their reality and contemporary power. If we really mean our confession then the grace of God is really there to release us from guilt and set us free to be the kind of person God wants us to be.

We don't need first to convince ourselves that we are monsters of depravity or to dredge around in our souls for sins to confess. We simply need to acknowledge what we have all experienced, the bind we are all in which was vividly described by St. Paul many years ago: ". . . though the will to do good is there, the deed is not. The good which I want to do, I fail to do; but what I do is the wrong which is against my will. . . ." "I discover this principle, then:" he goes on, "that when I want to do the right, only the wrong is within my reach. In my inmost self I delight in the law of God, but I perceive that there is in my bodily members a different law, fighting against the law that my reason approves and making me a prisoner. . . ." We know that kind of imprisonment, don't we? We just don't seem to be able to surmount these walls that shut us in with our own selfishness unless there is a helping hand. And that is just what the Gospel offers. "Who is there to rescue me? . . . God alone, through Jesus Christ our Lord!"

That is what is said to us every time we hear what is called the "Declaration of Pardon." That is what happens to us every time we open ourselves to the grace of God in private prayer, in reading the Bible, or in the traffic of every day. As another apostle put it: "If we claim to be sinless, we are self-deceived and stranger to the truth. If we confess our sins, he is just, and may be trusted to forgive our sins and cleanse us from every kind of wrong."

This is what I want to be talking about. At the moment it looks as though we are always talking about sins, not sin, and producing nothing but a guilty conscience about our failures and our follies. Surely what this generation needs is above all the note of grace that resounds whenever the church is healthy and alive. For that speaks of a forgiveness that reaches through to the root sin of our alienation from God and one another and a liberation and a reconciliation. A Christian is not one who stumbles around with a load of guilt which he tries to relieve by castigating other people's sins. He is one who has given up trying to justify himself before God or his fellowmen, who knows that he lives by grace and rejoices in the mercies of God "new every morning." There is no more liberating word in the whole world than that which is still spoken by Christ wherever there are ears to hear: "Your sins are forgiven . . . your faith has saved you . . . go in peace."

# I Wish Churches Would Mind Their Own Business

Something peculiar has been happening in the religious life of this country in the last ten years. What I have in mind is the curious paradox that while this has been a period of more and more activity for the churches in the social and political life of the nation, the polls show that most citizens think that their influence has been less and less. Just when churches have been intensely busy with all the questions that agitate the nation—race, peace, poverty, justice, and the like—people have been quietly deciding that they are having little effect. It is as though the more the church trumpets its concern the less the nation feels like paying attention.

Of course, it is extraordinarily difficult to gauge the impact of the church on any nation at any time. Its influence is not necessarily exerted through public pronouncements or pressure groups. The church is in action wherever a Christian man or woman is expressing an opinion, upholding an ideal, or working unobtrusively for a good cause. Yet it does seem at the moment as though many have decided that, in spite of its activism, or perhaps because of it, the institutional church is a declining power in the land.

This lies behind the remark that can be overheard in many quarters today: "I wish the churches would mind their own business." Those who express this opinion are telling us that the real business of the church is to convert men and women to Christianity and to nourish them in it. Then, if this were done effectively, the church would have a far greater influence on the nation than it does by joining in demonstrations, issuing pronouncements, and dabbling in politics, local, national, or international. Every time the mass media report the participation of clergy in a demonstration, or the arrest of a minister or priest, or a political pronouncement by a church council, I can almost overhear the grunts rising from a thousand breakfast tables: "I wish the churches would mind their own business."

Before we examine the validity of this point of view, I would remark that this is not the only opinion I overhear on this subject. Almost as often you can hear someone saying: "Why doesn't the church give a lead?" or "Why isn't the church more relevant to the real issues of today?" At the close of a meeting I once asked a group of students whether they thought the church should become more involved or less involved in social and political affairs. And about fifty percent cried "More!" while the other fifty percent cried "Less!" There is a deep

## I Wish Churches Would Mind Their Own Business

division in the nation and the church on this matter that could have serious consequences unless each side really tries to understand what the other is saying. "Give a lead" or "Mind your own business." These are the two denominations that threaten to come into being, for this division goes much deeper than the matters that separated us along the old denominational lines.

Let me try to listen hard to what is being said by those who are alarmed, distressed, or even infuriated by the church's intrusion into the social and political arena. The church's business, they would say, is to make Christians, not to tell me how to vote or to use my money for projects that seem to me to have little to do with the spreading of the Gospel. And they would point out that, while activist organizations abound today and much attention is being given to the problems of the secular world, very little is being done to train people in prayer, Bible reading, the spread of the Gospel, and preparation for the world to come. The common way to put it, both inside and outside the church, is that the first concern of the church is with the "spiritual," and not the material.

A recent and unexpected recruit to this position is Mr. Malcolm Muggeridge, the English essayist and critic. In a scathing attack on the activism of the modern churches he wrote recently: "It is natural enough, I suppose, that the churches in their

83

final decrepitude should thus concentrate on their social, and ignore their spiritual, responsibilities. Thereby they fall in with the prevailing temper of the age: everyone can understand the merit of giving a starving man food, or of championing the victims of napalm or apartheid, but the very language of mysticism or transcendentalism has ceased to be comprehensible . . . their better world promotion has the advantage of being a soft sell . . . even the saints have found Christian virtue hard to practice, but any tousled student can acquire a glow of righteousness by pouring a bucket of paint over some visiting speaker from the U.S. Embassy or South Africa House." (You can understand how this kind of remark makes Muggeridge an exciting if not always a popular visitor to British campuses!)

The point that is being made here seems to me worth listening to, whether we fully agree or not. There are all too evident signs of Christians capitulating to our secular culture and rejecting our heritage of faith in the unseen world. Not only do we have an emphasis today on the social and material consequences of our faith, but the faith itself is sometimes secularized. Put more simply this means that the man who says "My belief in God can only be expressed in social action" may soon go on to deny that he has any real God to believe in. It may be that some plunge into social action because they have given up the struggle to find a faith that really grips their minds and wills.

I suppose what is also in the minds of those who accuse the church of "meddling" is the apparent readiness of assemblies and councils to issue statements about matters beyond their technical competence or delicate political questions on which men of Christian goodwill are by no means agreed. I suppose the popular idea is that a group of clerics gather in some incense-filled room, concocting pronouncements out of a woolly idealism that is remote from the hard facts of life. Having occasionally sat on such committees, I must report that this picture is a caricature. Usually great care is taken to have expert laymen as members as well as ministers, and normally varying political points of view are represented. Yet I must confess that in recent years church bodies have seemed to me a little too ready to make public statements on thorny questions that require much thought and expertise, and on certain political matters to come down predictably on one side of the fence.

When, however, I overhear that the church should mind its own business, obviously more is being said than that the church should be careful in its pronouncements on social and political questions and less given to a militant activism. We are being told that the church should not be involved in such things at all. Suppose I were to ask "Just what *is* the church's business," the reply would probably be "To preach the Gospel and minister to our souls." The church is doing its own thing, in other words, if it confines itself to worship, evangelism, and the promotion of personal piety. Everything else —war, poverty, race, birth control, abortion, housing, matters of government—should be left to the individual conscience of the believer.

This sounds quite a reasonable proposition, until we begin to reflect a little on recent history. We shall then discover that this conception of the church's business is the one held by totalitarian powers. Pastor Niemoeller once told me of an interview he had with Hitler, who raved against the church's interference in social and political matters. "You can deal with heaven," he said, "the German people on earth belong to me." This is also the Communist position. Churches in the Soviet orbit are normally free to conduct worship as they please, but there is severe restriction on any social activity, and pronouncements affecting state policy are out of the question, unless they happen to coincide with the party line. We cannot blame Christians in Germany for acquiescing in the Nazi takeover, if we believe that the church should be entirely unconcerned with affairs of state. The anti-Nazi Confessional Church in Germany was not primarily concerned with political action, but they saw the implications of some Nazi policies and were bold enough to con-

I WISH CHURCHES WOULD MIND THEIR OWN BUSINESS

demn them openly. Would anyone want to say now that a church that condemned anti-Semitism in Nazi Germany was not minding its own business and should have kept quiet?

You see, it is not possible to draw a firm line and say "The church's business ends here." For me there is no question about our primary duty to preach the Gospel and offer worship to almighty God. If that is not central then the church might as well go out of business altogether for many of the other things could be better done by secular agencies. But preaching the Gospel is not something that concerns only the soul of man. Jesus Christ came in the flesh, and he was concerned with every aspect of man's life, physical as well as spiritual. And worship is not something that happens in a vacuum. It is an offering of the total life of men and women to God in Christ. If it is the church's business to bring to men and women the Word of God, would it not also be its business to try to feed them if they were starving? And if, as most would admit, we have this duty of care for their bodies, does this not also extend to the body politic where decisions are made affecting human welfare? There is a big difference between political action for its own sake and political action taken for the sake of the Gospel.

The younger generation today is very skeptical about an institution that proclaims the validity and necessity of Christian love but refuses to say anything or do anything about social conditions that are a denial of that love. They may be often reckless in their demands, unfair in their criticism, and unthinking in their demands on the church, but we must remember how difficult it is for them to believe that the church means business in this question of Christian love if we seem to care little about such matters as justice, economic opportunity, housing, or racial prejudice. The Hebrew prophets were not slow to denounce a purely "spiritual" worship that neglected the physical problems on the church's doorstep. "Hear this word of the Lord," says Amos. "Take thou away from me the noise of thy songs; for I will not hear the melody of thy viols. But let judgment run down as waters, and righteousness as a mighty stream." In modern terms that would mean: "I don't want to hear your lovely hymns or glorious pipe organs unless you are concerned with justice and fair play in the community."

It would be tragic if the rift in the church between what are called "activists" and "pietists" got any wider. For surely any true follower of Christ must see that an extreme position on this matter will betray the Gospel. If being an "activist" means that I neglect my prayers, minimize my worship, and cease to believe in the eternal dimension, then I have parted company with the New Testament altogether. On the other hand, if being a pietist means that I think of the Gospel as a purely spiritual trans-

## I Wish Churches Would Mind Their Own Business

action between my soul and God with no obligations on my conduct as a citizen, then this is equally a betrayal of the message of Christ. Similarly, if the church were to turn away from its worship and evangelism and devote itself entirely to involvement in the social and political questions of the day, it would cease to be the church of Jesus Christ, while, if it completely rejected all such involvement it would be disobedient to its Lord, and in effect denying the message of the Incarnation—that the Word was made flesh.

So I would want to plead for mutual understanding. To those who are impatient with the reluctance of our churches to identify themselves at once with every cause that seems to represent peace, justice, and social betterment, I would say "All right. We have been often too slow and often too timid; but at times we may have also been too fast and too bold. How many today would say without hesitation that those churches in the thirties who identified themselves with prohibition and pacifism were right? And, most important of all, how can the churches have any real impact on social conditions if we lose the one thing that is our unique motivation, the reconciling Gospel of Jesus Christ?"

To those who are aghast at what looks to them like a disastrous swing away from the church's main business to a meddling with mundane affairs, I would say: "Your word of warning is needed in

OVERHEARD

these days of increasing secularism and disbelief in the central truths of the Gospel; but surely you don't mean that a church should have no concern about, for instance, the ghettoes of our cities and what causes them, the proportion of public money spent on armaments, or the rights and wrongs of birth control and abortion? Surely you don't mean that the church should keep silent if any power should seem to be threatening our human liberties or refuse to comment on trends that threaten the moral fiber of the nation?"

There is surely a meeting ground for Christians of different temperaments here, and the church should be a place where we can speak of these things to one another in love. Let's agree that the church should mind its own business, but the church's business is both narrow and wide. It is narrow as it concentrates on that commitment to Christ that leads to life eternal; it is wide enough to cover, in Christ's name, the whole area of our mortal life.

# Religion Is for the Weak: I Don't Need a Savior

Suppose we listen to what is probably the most powerful argument against religion that is circulating today. It is openly and sometimes brutally expressed by a few brilliant writers, but its echoes can be overheard wherever the question of faith is seriously discussed. And you can catch the whispers of it in every corner of the modern world. The essence of it is that a mature man standing on his own two feet doesn't need any religion to help him through life, and that religion is an illusion developed for the comfort and reassurance of the weak.

I said this is a powerful argument because it does in fact influence so many people. It is not a compelling argument in itself. For the truth or falsehood of religion doesn't depend on whether we need it or not. If I feel the need of God in my life that is no proof that he is really there, but similarly if I don't happen to feel that need that is no proof that he is not there. To tell me that my religion is an illusion simply because I find in it a strength and satisfaction is like telling a child that his love for his parents is an illusion because it fulfills a real need. We shall not discover the truth about God simply by arguing over our needs and hopes.

However, the accusation stands: "Religion is for the weak: I don't need a Savior," and multitudes are impressed by it. Last century, the philosopher Nietzsche attacked what he called the "slave-morality" of Christians and exalted the superman who accepts responsibility for his own actions and is accountable to no one. A whole generation was impressed by the thought of humanity throwing off the shackles of dependence upon God and facing its destiny as free beings. Bertrand Russell gave this philosophy its most eloquent expression when he wrote of man now facing the grim truth that there is no God directing our affairs and no eternal life to look forward to. He spoke of man's "origin, his growth, his hopes and fears, his loves and his beliefs," as being no more than "the outcome of accidental collocations of atoms." His grim conclusion was that "all the labors of the ages, all the devotion, all the inspiration, all the noonday brightness of human genius, are destined to extinction in the vast death of the solar system, and that the whole temple of man's achievement must inevitably be buried beneath the debris of a universe in ruins"; and concluded that "only within the scaffolding of these truths, only on the firm foundation of unyielding despair, can the soul's habitation be safely built."

This is, if you like, a sermon in reverse. It is a

Religion Is for the Weak: I Don't Need a Savior

moving proclamation of disbelief in any God or any Savior for the human race. Not many have followed Russell down this path of "unyielding despair," but the suggestion that the really strong man or woman can have no alternative is with us yet. We hear much today about the coming of age of the human race, about our ability to dispense with the props of religions, and many simply write off religion as a relic of man's primitive feeling of weakness facing a hostile universe. Religion is called a "culture lag," on its way to extinction. Occasionally this is linked to our scientific progress, as when the Provost of King's College, Cambridge, in England, said in a recent broadcast, "Men have become like gods. Isn't it about time we understood our divinity? Science offers us total mastery over our environment and over our destiny . . . all of us need to understand that God, or nature, or change, or evolution, or the course of history, or whatever you like to call it, can't be trusted any more. We simply *must* take charge of our own fate."

I sometimes think we need a statement like this from an academic really to realize how absurd this notion of man's omnipotence really is. For who, when he really thinks it through, can accept the proposition that we are being offered "total mastery over our environment and destiny"? No one is more amazed or impressed than I am at the astounding achievements of modern science, but I have never yet met

OVERHEARD

a scientist who would claim that we are on our way to this sort of total mastery. Indeed, it is even more obvious that precisely the same moral flaws that haunted our ancestors are with us in the age of technology—the only difference being that our moral weakness today carries infinitely more dangerous consequences for the human race. So far are we from total mastery that we are desperately striving to prevent our technology from becoming the instrument of mass destruction. Scientists have shown themselves especially sensitive to this moral weakness of humanity, and would be the last to claim that our vast increase in knowledge and control of the physical universe have made us fit to behave as gods. I should also want to ask who the "we" are who are going to take charge of our fate. Almost certainly not you and I and the man next door. The threat here is of the emergence of an elite who will play God in our world and decide what is best for the human race. No, man has undoubtedly grown up in his understanding of the universe, but there is no sign whatever that he has overcome the tragic flaw in his nature that reveals his weakness, his need of some rescuing power.

But I don't want to base my reply to the man who thinks religion the refuge of the weak simply on a reminder that with all our progress we *are* weak. Many of us resent the kind of preacher who tries, as it were, to catch us in a moment of anxiety or

RELIGION IS FOR THE WEAK: I DON'T NEED A SAVIOR

despair. Dietrich Bonhoeffer tells us in one of his letters from prison how he despised the technique of striking at a man with our religion when his defenses are down. When allied planes were bombing Berlin and he found himself locked in his prison with other men during these pulverizing raids, he deliberately refused to take advantage of their fear by offering them the consolations of religion. I've often wondered if he was right—it seems almost a betrayal of his duty as a preacher of the Gospel—yet I can see how he felt. The Gospel, he believed, is directed to the whole of man at all times and is not to be thought of as an emergency supply or an escape hatch when the going gets rough. In other words, it should be a first and not a last resort. So if I heard a man declare "Religion is for the weak: I don't need a Savior," I would rather reply to him right there and then, than wait till some tragedy hit him so that I could then produce the consolations of religion. In army terms it's not fox-hole religion that counts so much as plain, everyday barrack-room religion.

What, then, is the answer to give to the confident, healthy, self-possessed man or woman who has written off religion as the refuge of the weak?

I would be inclined at first to query this way of putting it. There is indeed a fundamental difference of attitude to life between the genuinely religious and the genuinely irreligious, but does it lie in the

OVERHEARD

fact that one is weak and the other is strong? The critic points to some notorious weak and timid souls he knows and says: "These people just have to have a crutch to lean on. They're just not mature enough to go it alone." And he may point to our fondness for hymns like "Jesus, Lover of My Soul, Let Me to Thy Bosom Fly," or "Rock of Ages, Cleft for Me, Let Me Hide Myself in Thee." But I would immediately ask whether religion should be judged by those who use it as a mere refuge from the storm or by its strongest exponents, its leaders, its saints, and its scholars. Would anyone want to say that this Dietrich Bonhoeffer, who went to his death on the order of Hitler with a radiant confidence that impressed both friend and foe, was a weak man? Was Martin Luther King, practicing nonviolent resistance, a weak character? To go farther back, what about Calvin, Luther, Aquinas, St. Francis of Assisi, Augustine, Paul—are these weak, timid, clinging, helpless people? And what about the One whom Christians are called to follow, the One who is their ideal of a human being as well as their divine Lord? Was this a weak character who set his face to go to Jerusalem and accept the horrors that awaited him there? Was this a weak man who, when overwhelmed with the evil that surrounded him, was able to say after praying for an escape: "Nevertheless, not my will but thine be done"?

The more we think about it, the more we ponder

RELIGION IS FOR THE WEAK: I DON'T NEED A SAVIOR

the lives of the truly religious and the irreligious people we have known, the clearer it is that the difference between them cannot be described in these terms. What is it then? I believe it to be the difference, not between the weak and the strong, but between the humble and the proud. The true remark to make would be, not "Religion is for the weak; I don't need a Savior," but "Religion is for the humble; I'm too proud to want a Savior."

The moment I say this I realize that I am on dangerous ground. For pride is a slippery thing, and it would be quite easy to start boasting about one's humility. Certainly a religious person is not one who goes around saying: "I'm much more humble than you." But if we forget about ourselves for a moment and think of the really good people we have known, we must be struck by an element of real humility in their make-up. It's this kind of humility—an openness, a teachability, a readiness to listen, a sensitivity to others—that Christ spoke of when he said: "Blessed are the meek: for they shall inherit the earth." The proud are the ones who miss the inheritance, for they are so wrapped up in their own concerns, their own ambitions, their own opinions, that their souls are closed to what could come from outside.

Jesus never suggested that the essence of religion was weakness, but he told lots of stories that revealed the difference between the humble attitude and the proud. The root of it all is in the little tale of the two men praying. One "stood and prayed thus with himself," we read (note "with himself"!) "God, I thank thee that I am not as other men are. . . ." The other, you remember, "smote upon his breast, saying, God be merciful to me a sinner."

This is why Jesus so often spoke of the child as the clue to real religion. He was not commending childishness, but that openness, freshness, dependence, and teachability that is the mark of the infant. That is the spirit we find in the most remarkable religious leaders of history and of today. They may be tough administrators, brilliant scholars, or soaring mystics, but all have an essential humility that looks to God as a child to a father. And the anonymous Christians of whom the world has never heard are marked by this same characteristic—they know of their ignorance, their faults, and their weaknesses, and they look for the wisdom, the forgiveness, and the strength that flow from the Grace of God.

Religion for the weak? Yes, in the sense that we all share in the fundamental human weaknesses—pride, folly, fear, despair. But it comes alive only when humility gives the grace of God the opening to supply what we lack and empower us from a source beyond ourselves. "I don't need a Savior"? Then you have reserves within you to conquer this pride, folly, fear, and despair?

The more sensitive we are to the desperate needs

of our modern world, the less we are hypnotized by the triumphs of technology, the more likely we are to recognize that man's fundamental needs are what they have been since the beginning. Of course we have no time for a whining, grovelling religion, but neither has the Bible. Let me conclude with two incidents, one from the Old Testament and one from the New, to illustrate what I mean.

Here is religion in action as a decisive moment in Israel's history. The Hebrews have escaped from Egypt and stand trembling by the Red Sea; for already Pharaoh's horses and chariots are in hot pursuit. A time for prayer we would say, and that's what Moses thought. Well, if you think the Bible is full of foxhole religion listen to the words that Moses heard from the Lord: "Wherefore criest thou unto me? Speak unto the children of Israel, that they go forward." The man who heard that Voice was no snivelling weakling, but he had the humility to trust in his Lord and go forward.

In the New Testament we find St. Paul worrying about his thorn in the flesh. Whatever it was it represented a weakness either in the flesh or in the soul. And he prays with the humility of one who knows his own limits. "For this thing," he says, "I besought the Lord thrice, that it might depart from me." And what happened? Here is the secret of true religion—not an escape but an armament. "He said unto me, My grace is sufficient for thee: for my strength is made perfect in weakness." It was in that strength that this amazing man was able to face mob violence, shipwreck, floggings, and imprisonment and write at the end of it all: "I can do all things through Christ who strengthens me."

The next time you overhear the remark that religion is for the weak think of Moses, think of Paul, think above all of Jesus Christ in whose humiliation we find our divine companion and in whose Resurrection our immortal strength.

# I've Tried Prayer and It Doesn't Work

Sometimes I feel that I don't want ever again to talk about prayer. And that's not because as a minister I've done too much talking but because I've not done enough praying. If there's one topic about which one should stop talking and get on with it, it's prayer. In the average church today it is much easier to get a group together to discuss prayer than to practice it. If I've any excuse for discussing it with you now, it is in the hope that what I say might encourage someone to begin again or to put some new energy into what so easily becomes a dead routine.

Why I hesitate to speak about it is that prayer is essentially talking *with* God, not *about* God and what he might do for us. If that seems obvious I can't help remarking that a great deal that is called public prayer today seems to be directed much more to an audience than to the Lord. We clergy are guilty of using words and phrases designed to rouse the attention of the human hearers rather than God's, if I may put it that way. We even preach at people through our prayers, completely forgetting to whom

OVERHEARD

we are talking. A newspaper once reported that a certain prayer was "the finest ever addressed to a Boston audience." I wonder if God thought it was equally fine? True prayer is not a statement, however important, but a communion with God. I have heard preachers offer the Lord a lecture in theology or a review of the international situation when all he wanted was surely a shout of praise or a cry for help.

Another caveat is needed when we talk about prayer. We too easily find that our head is at war with our heart. What I mean is that for most of us prayer is quite natural and instinctive, while the moment we stop to think about it and discuss the implications of what we are doing, we get bamboozled to the point where the head begins to tell the heart that it's no use. So we have the odd situation that almost everybody in this country probably prays at some time or another while very few can give any fully convincing reason for doing so. (Opinion polls have revealed the surprising fact that even people who say they don't believe in God admit that they pray!) Sometimes it's better just to let the heart speak even if the head is raising objections. However, today I must face the biggest mental block of all, the one that often persuades people to stifle the instinct of the heart. In crude terms, such as we might overhear any day of the week: "I've tried prayer, and it doesn't work."

## I'VE TRIED PRAYER AND IT DOESN'T WORK

Now, of course, there's a way of saying this that is hard to take seriously. A child might say: "I put a big empty box by my bed and prayed that God would fill it with dollar bills, and he didn't." "I tried this prayer for a week, and it didn't work." We don't need to be experts in theology to see that this is not an argument against prayer but against magic. Yet it's not only children who cling to the idea that prayer is chiefly a way of obtaining some personal advantage in a miraculous way. Adults can be equally obtuse and sometimes rule prayer out of their lives for no better reason than that their requests for some personal advantage have not been immediately granted.

My task would be comparatively easy if everyone who says prayer doesn't work had this superstitious conception of what it is. But I am forced to recognize that many people who have given up faith in prayer have had much more serious reasons for doing so. Behind the remark "I've tried prayer, and it doesn't work" may lie the agony of a searing experience when fervent prayer was offered for the recovery of one's dearest, and there was none. Or perhaps a passionate prayer for the overcoming of a recurring temptation has seemed to be totally unanswered. And what about the parents who have prayed daily for their children since infancy and yet seen them grow up apparently unresponsive to their God? It's not the frivolous objection that I

OVERHEARD

have in mind today, but the terrible, numbing conclusion to which a man or woman may be driven by sad experience, "I've tried prayer, and it doesn't work." There are probably far more people who have felt like this than ever say it out loud.

Yes, there are standard answers to this complaint: "You didn't pray hard enough or often enough or with enough faith." Or, "You were too demanding, not submissive enough to God's will." None of these is very convincing if we have been told from childhood that God is the one who hears and answers prayer. The Bible doesn't surround the promise with a forest of conditions. We are told simply to ask and it will be given us. And both the Old and New Testaments are full of examples of people praying in dozens of different ways, from the most spontaneous to the most formal, and with many shades of faith and conviction. They whisper, they shout, they demand, they cajole, they commune, they complain, they accept. We can get lots of insights from a study of these Bible prayers. One thing we cannot get is a set of rules. Prayer in the Bible is an intensely human thing, and I would never suggest to a baffled and disappointed man or woman that there was something wrong with their technique.

What, then, *is* wrong when I pray and nothing seems to happen?

Nothing is wrong, I would say, except giving up. We all know that Christ made some very categorical

## I'VE TRIED PRAYER AND IT DOESN'T WORK

statements about prayer: ". . . Ask, and it shall be given you; seek, and ye shall find; knock, and it shall be opened unto you"; "If ye shall ask anything in my name, I will do it." These are the very sayings that seem to mock us when our prayers seem to hit an unresponsive ceiling and drop back unanswered. But Christ said something else that we may have missed. The astonishing story about the widow who pestered a corrupt judge till she won her case is prefaced by the words: "He spake a parable unto them to this end, that men ought always to pray, and not to faint." This is one of the places where the King James version blunts the impact for us today. (I remember hearing this verse as a boy and wondering how passing out cold on the floor could be an alternative to praying!) The New English Bible reads: "He spoke to them in a parable to show that they should keep on praying and never lose heart." "Never lose heart"—it seems to me that these words are spoken directly to the one who says in real distress: "I've tried praying, and it doesn't work."

Our Lord evidently knew that we are all going to be tempted at some time to lose heart, to give up praying. He was well aware that the explicit promises he was giving about prayer would make it all the more difficult for us to carry on when they did not seem to be fulfilled. He himself facing the horrors of arrest and the subsequent brutalities prayed,

"Father, if thou be willing, remove this cup from me." And there seemed to be no answer beyond the rustling of the leaves in the trees of Gethsemane. Then, we read that "being in an agony he prayed more earnestly." It is this man with this experience of the hideous silence of the heavens who tells us that we should keep on praying and never lose heart. What were his last words as he drank the cup to the last bitter dregs and was dying on the Cross? "I've tried prayer, and it doesn't work"? "Father," he said, "into thy hands I commend my spirit."

What this says to me is that when we are crushed by the apparent ineffectiveness of our prayers we are not to ask ourselves "Where did I go wrong?" or conclude that, after all, our petitions were wasted breath. Our only error will be to stop praying. "Keep on praying," said the one who did it, "and never lose heart." Somehow I can't imagine one of the disciples looking into the eyes of Jesus and saying "Lord, I've tried prayer, and it doesn't work." They may have felt that way, as we do, from time to time, but when they found themselves in his presence what they said was "Lord, teach us to pray." I think it will be like that with us. The closer we come to Christ, the more we soak ourselves in the records of his life and his teaching the less likely we are to feel that our experience of prayer is sufficient for us to draw the conclusion that "it doesn't work." Rather will we begin to realize how little we know

## I'VE TRIED PRAYER AND IT DOESN'T WORK

about this tremendous and mysterious activity, and we would want to say: "Lord, I've hardly begun to understand what prayer means and sometimes I am baffled and disappointed. Lord, for you it seems so fresh, so new, so powerful, so infinitely real. Lord, teach me to pray."

Part of our trouble about prayer not working comes from our assumption that we know what it is. If we know all about it, then we can be in a position to pronounce the judgment: "It doesn't work."

Suppose a man decides to take up the game of golf and gets the necessary equipment. Then he buys a little book that explains how to swing the clubs and send the ball soaring away toward the green. He now knows all about it, and there he is standing on the tee ready to drive. He does all the little book required: slowly the club goes back and keeping his eye fastened on the ball and his head well down, he brings it whistling down—smack! A piece of turf flies into the air and the ball is still sitting there grinning at him. So he flings his clubs away, tears up his little book, and strides away saying, "Golf! I've tried it, and it doesn't work!" If we are golfers we may have felt like that, but somehow we stay around and watch while someone comes up, does all the things we thought we were doing, and cracks that ball smoothly straight down the middle of the fairway. And we catch on that there is something we have yet to learn.

OVERHEARD

Have you ever thought how odd it was for men who had been taught to pray at their mother's knee, who had learned and repeated the prayers of the synagogue, who almost certainly prayed three times a day without fail, to say to Jesus, "Teach us to pray"? It makes us feel that prayer as Christ knew it and practiced it and taught it must be something vaster than we know, a spiritual ingredient of life that we have hardly begun to explore. So instead of thinking that we've really tried it and found it useless, we might well ask if we've done more than dabble with it up to now.

That, at least, is how I feel when I compare my own praying with that of Christ or of the spiritual athletes of the church. But I hope nobody thinks that I am despising the simple prayers of the average man and suggesting that only an elite know what prayer really is. All I am doing is to confess that you and I are beginners in this dimension of life and hardly in a position to judge whether or not "it works."

Just what do we mean, indeed, by saying that prayer works or doesn't work? Not much more surely than that I asked God for "x" to happen and either it did or it didn't. On the basis of believers and unbelievers one can argue forever; like millions of other Christians I can tell of times when a definite prayer for "x" to happen was granted in a remarkable way. And I can tell of other times it wasn't. But

## I'VE TRIED PRAYER AND IT DOESN'T WORK

even though this may be one of the lower levels of prayer, I'll still go on making specific requests. The skeptic, of course, can smile at what I call an "answer." There is always some alternative explanation for what happens. But I go on believing that there is a connection between what happened and my prayers.

But what is the connection? This is where we get beyond the notion that prayer "works" in the same kind of way that flipping a switch works to turn the lights on. I dislike all mechanical illustrations of prayer because it is something intensely personal. Fundamentally it is the relating of my will to God's will. If God's will is always for an ultimate good, for what the Bible calls our "salvation," which simply means total health, mental, physical, and spiritual, then in prayer my will becomes a channel through which his will can work. If we were automatons and this world merely a mechanical system, God's will would use us as such a channel. But because we have mysterious freedom, this choice between good and evil, the good and saving will of God works through his communication with his human family.

If, then, prayer is not just "asking God for something" but the time we spend alone with him speaking and seeking to let his will be done in us and through us, then it always "works." Even when a prayer was a desperate pleading for a life to be saved, and it didn't happen, that prayer was not

OVERHEARD

empty and lost. I'm not saying that we have to accept what happens as the will of God. I don't believe it is the will of God that children should starve to death in Africa or young men should die in Vietnam. The mystery of evil is too deep, the love of God too great for any such conclusion. But I am saying that our genuine prayers work at all times in all places. For the strong truth to grasp in this most agonizing of our experiences is the Bible's assurance that "God works in all things for good with them that love him." All things that happen are not necessarily good in his sight. Jesus didn't think it good that the widow's son should die. God didn't think it good that a child should perish. But he *works* in all things for good with them that love him.

To pray is to show that we love him. Then, as we pray, he works. "I've tried prayer, and it doesn't work." Perhaps not, but if it was real prayer *he* does.

# I'll Take Christian Ethics but Not the Fairy Tales

Every year as the Christmas season comes around the churches are apt to get into a losing battle. They fight to make Christmas a religious festival, a time of holy joy, of worship and meditation on the mystery of the Incarnation. With salvos of sermons, slogans like "Keep Christ in Christmas," the churches campaign against the secularization of the holy season. But the public in general is unimpressed. The holy day has become a holiday, and the barrage of religious propaganda is not likely to turn the clock back. John Q. Citizen may sympathize generally with the church's cause, but he continues to treat Christmas as a jolly midwinter break, an occasion for swapping gifts and Santa Claus, time for the kids. Worship comes pretty low on his list (unless there's something cozy going on with trees, candles, and children's voices), and he's not going to be found doing much pondering on the doctrine of the Incarnation.

I call this a losing battle because I don't see how we can expect those who have no vital belief in the Gospel of the Son of God becoming man for our sal-

OVERHEARD

vation suddenly to find it true and exciting on the 25th of December. You can't force people to celebrate something they don't really believe, and I see no reason to grudge the secular world its enjoyment of a festival that originated in the church. Only if it became completely paganized would I feel that the church would have to pull out of the whole affair and concentrate on its own unique celebration. After all, as the old Puritans who did just that used to point out, there is nothing about Christmas in the Bible, and the evidence is that the origins of the feast go back a long way before the birth of Christ.

Would I be wrong in estimating that today a minority celebrate Christmas because it is the festival of the birth of their Lord and Savior, that a smaller minority reject Christmas because they are violently opposed to all such religious belief, and that the big majority indulge in a pagan Christmas with a sympathetic glance at its religious meaning and perhaps a nostalgic wish that they could believe it to be true?

It's this silent majority, to use a fashionable phrase, that I am talking about. The totally convinced Christians are vocal at this season. We sing our carols and tell the Christmas story and proclaim by word and Sacrament what we believe, the astonishing report of God's word that he "was made flesh and dwelt among us." The militant atheists and secularists trumpet their disbelief and try to eliminate

## I'LL TAKE CHRISTIAN ETHICS BUT NOT THE FAIRY TALES

all traces of what they call "superstition" from the holiday season. But the middle is silent on the religious issue. There is a large reservoir of respect for Christianity, or at least for its founder. Some are prompted to attend worship, as at Easter, from some decent instinct of gratitude or respect for ancestral tradition or perhaps even hope that religion could become real again. But it's not a time for exposing their doubts and reservations about Christian beliefs. They have no desire to disturb the satisfaction of those who still believe, and they are more than aware of the value of the Christian ethic in our time.

So, from the silent middle, this is what I overhear, "I'll take Christian ethics but not the fairy tales." I overhear because not too many talk as bluntly as this, especially to a minister. But this is surely what it amounts to: A great many of our contemporaries would like to be thought Christian because they believe in what they would call the "ideals of Christianity" and the way of life it stands for, but they balk at the religious bit, the personal God whose Son came to earth, the notion of salvation as some kind of mystical experience. It is particularly the miracles which seem still to be tied up with it all.

Often when this point of view is expressed today the speaker feels very up-to-date. He implies that, of course, the religious bit was all right for his grandparents, but today we've got to have a secularized, scientific outlook, and that includes ethics but ex-

113

cludes this religious thing. The fact is, of course, that the attempt to separate Christian ethics from Christian theology goes back about 1900 years. It was particularly popular in the eighteenth century when brilliant books were written in the effort to preserve Christian morality while dispensing with all supernatural impedimenta, especially miracles. You could certainly have provoked a debate among the founding fathers of the Republic on this very subject.

No, this remark, "I'll take Christian ethics but not the fairy tales," is so far from being a shocking expression of modernity that it is already somewhat out-of-date. What I mean is that the experience of recent years has shown thoughtful observers that the notion you can simply abstract Christian religion for Christian ethics is false. Both believers and unbelievers are now more likely to agree that the theology and the ethics belong together. So today the battle is on the whole front. The more radical critics are not just rejecting what they call the "fairy tales," they are rejecting or seriously questioning the ethics too. And the believer is more and more aware that without a solid structure of religious belief, there is no power or stability in any system of Christian morals.

Whether we like it or not, then, Christian morals and Christian religious beliefs are tied together. It's possible for the morals to endure for a generation or two after the beliefs have evaporated. Many of us

## I'll Take Christian Ethics but Not the Fairy Tales

can think of men and women of what we would call outstandingly Christian character who profess no commitment to the Christian faith. Often you will find that the faith was strongly there in the homes from which they came. For a true religion will go on producing fruit just as flowers will bloom in a bowl for days after they have been cut. But the signs are that this situation will not last. Ours has, in fact, been called a "cut-flower" Christian civilization just because there is no longer a strong supporting and surrounding faith to nourish the Christian way of life.

We have only to think what it means to say "I'll take Christian ethics." Do we really think that it's so easy? I'm always astonished at the man who says he lives by the simple code of the Sermon on the Mount. There has been only one man in history who has totally lived it out, and he was crucified. The rest of us, if we take Christian ethics seriously, know how very far short we continually fall and are sooner or later driven to ask, "Is there no power beyond myself that can lift me up towards this level? Is there any way in which my miserable selfishness and folly can be transcended? Is there a hope of a forgiveness by which I can continually make a new start?" As soon as we ask this kind of question we are in the sphere of religion, of faith in God.

Right, someone may want to say, but there's a difference between what you call faith in God and

OVERHEARD

what I call "fairy tales." I can respect a belief in a divine power we can draw on but the Christian church asks me to swallow entirely too much. What about all this stuff about a Son of God coming down from heaven? What do you expect me to make of angels, devils, and miracles in this world of moon shots, heart transplants, and nuclear power?

Let me try to answer this objection with three brief comments.

1. First, if by "fairy tales" is meant stories about miraculous happenings that strain our credulity, the New Testament contains remarkably few. And the miracles that are recorded are not presented as magic events to impress the reader. Every one of them carries some deep meaning connected with the person of Christ. If you want to know how restrained the Gospels are in reporting miracles, you have only to read some of the books that circulated about Jesus that were not admitted into our Bible. For instance, there is one that contains a story about Jesus as a boy. He makes some little clay pigeons, then he claps his hands and they all become real pigeons and fly away. That's what I mean by a "fairy tale." Such a miracle is just a piece of magic and tells us nothing true or helpful about Jesus Christ. Compare that with the kind of miracle the Gospels record—the healings, the feeding of the crowds, the stilling of the storm, even the walking on the water —and you will note that your attention is always

## I'LL TAKE CHRISTIAN ETHICS BUT NOT THE FAIRY TALES

drawn from the actual miracle to the underlying meaning that has to do with our understanding of Christ. We can also keep in mind that some things that looked like miracles then are understandable to us in psychological terms, and the possibility that on occasion a natural event was interpreted as a miracle by those who recorded it. But I would not want to strip the Bible of this miraculous element altogether. There are strange things recorded. What strikes the careful reader is that compared with other writings of the time the note of the miraculous is remarkably restrained and concentrates on the person of Jesus Christ.

2. So the second thing I want to say is: Why worry about some incidents you find it hard to accept when the whole point of the Gospel's records is to present you with one supreme miracle, one stupendous, almost incredible event, that God himself became man in Jesus Christ. The last of the four Gospels is quite frank about the purpose of these books: "These things are written, that ye might believe that Jesus is the Christ, the Son of God; and that believing ye might have life through his name." Christ himself is the supreme miracle. And when we come to believe in him and receive that amazing new life, I don't see why we should worry any more about the few stories that speak of strange happenings connected with his life. I should rather find it surprising if when this unique Person was

OVERHEARD

active among us nothing out of the ordinary took place. So you will see that there's not much point arguing about the so-called "fairy tales" unless we come to grips with the central claim of Christianity —that God was in this Man reconciling the world to himself. The Gospels bring us this story of the Incarnation, and it is crowned by the ultimate miracle of the Resurrection. Those who receive this Christ and know that he is alive have experienced a miracle in their own lives. We cannot pretend it is otherwise. We don't want to explain it away. After all, even the disciples when they first heard the news of the Resurrection dismissed the story as a fairy tale. St. Luke tells us that when the women told them about Jesus being alive again "their words seemed to them as idle tales, and they believed them not." It's not just our generation that find such a miracle hard to accept. The Gospel of Christ is not a moral platitude. The Good News is not ordinary news. It challenges our faith until like Thomas we stretch out our unbelieving hands and say: "My Lord and my God."

3. And that leads me to the last point. Are we not now coming to a time when the world of mystery, the dimension of the eternal, is once again coming into its own. The signs are that people are more and more disenchanted with the search for purely secular solutions to our problems, with a life lived only on the plane of the thoroughly natural and understandable. So perhaps we shall be less likely

## I'll Take Christian Ethics but Not the Fairy Tales

in the future to use words like "fairy tales" to dismiss all that is not immediately understandable and reducible to scientific terms. We are realizing that all ethical systems including the Christian need the backing of a faith that reaches beyond this material world and offers us the resources of a divine dimension. So to the one who says "I'll take Christian ethics but not the fairy tales," I would quote Hamlet's remark to his friend:

> There are more things in heaven and earth, Horatio,
> Than are dreamt of in your philosophy . . .

and I would pray that among "these things" he would discover the presence of the living Christ.

# I Suppose Christ Is
# Really a Kind of Myth

Just suppose for a moment that our Christmas star this year took the form of a genuine flying saucer with some cosmic visitors on board. It lands in some remote corner of the Rockies, and out of it steps a little exploring party from some distant planet. The visitors are not only what we call "intelligent creatures." but are from a civilization some thousands of years in advance of ours. They have studied our language and have acquired a method of rapid individual transportation, every man his own jet, so that they can reach our big cities quickly. Most surprising of all is that they have learned the art of invisibility at will so that they wander freely through our streets, travel our buses and subways, enter our homes, restaurants, and clubs, experience our football games, our church services, our demonstrations, and our Christmas parties. They take notes everywhere and by mid-January are whizzing off to their home planet with enough material for a thousand page report on "The Habits and Beliefs of the American Section of the Natives on Planet Earth."

I want to turn to the chapter of that report labeled

## I Suppose Christ Is Really a Kind of Myth

"Religion." And what I find myself reading is something like this: "Our expedition to America coincided with an annual celebration called Christmas. For a period of weeks culminating on the 25th of December on their calendar the natives decorate their homes and public buildings, organize social events of various kinds, especially for children, exchange gifts, and constantly wish one another happiness and merriment. We had not thought to include this celebration in our chapter on religion until we noticed the constant recurrence of certain symbols, a star, a child's cradle, a tree, and concluded that these had some religious significance. Then we found that at the climax of the festival the churches were unusually active and seemed, indeed, to claim some sort of monopoly on its meaning. Further investigation elicited the information that a 'mass' is a church celebration and 'Christ' is the name of the God who is worshipped in these churches, hence Christ-mas, Christmas. This Christ is a name of great power and influence with many Americans, but we found it difficult in listening to conversations to discover just who he was, or is. Some talk as though he were a great folk hero of the past whose teachings were well in advance of his time and who was brutally executed by his contemporaries. Others talk as though he were still somehow alive and find some deeper meaning in his execution which they symbolize by a Cross. The majority, however, seemed rather confused about this and on

OVERHEARD

one occasion at least we overheard the remark: 'I suppose Christ is really a kind of myth.' We suggest that a second expedition give some study to this remarkable phenomenon."

So much for the fantasy. All I'm really concerned with now is the popular response to Christmas and the overheard remark that Christ is some kind of myth. When the average man without any strong religious convictions thinks about the meaning of the carols or the Nativity narratives, he is almost bound to come up with the idea of myth. Obviously much more is being celebrated than the birth of a good man. "The Brightness of glory, Light of light eternal, Our lowly nature he hath not abhorred: Son of the Father, Word of God Incarnate! O come, let us adore him, Christ, the Lord!" (I've always thought it wonderful that the most popular carols are those that contain the toughest theology, but I doubt if much of it is inwardly digested with our Christmas fare!) "Veiled in flesh the Godhead see; Hail the Incarnate Deity. . . ." "And the Word was made flesh and dwelt among us, (and we beheld his glory, the glory as of the only begotten of the Father), full of grace and truth." The only way the average thinking man or woman outside or sometimes inside the church can make sense of these assertions is to use the notion of myth.

But what exactly is a myth? In popular speech a myth is often little more than a polite name for a

## I Suppose Christ Is Really a Kind of Myth

lie or what some people call a non-event, something that didn't happen. A myth is little Tommy telling you that he saw a great red dragon with a princess in its claws outside the supermarket. But scholars have a different way of using the word. Technically it means a tale that is told to convey or illustrate some truth or arouse certain emotions. The myths of ancient Egypt or Greece, for example, were of this kind; and every society right to the present day has created its myths. Recently there has been a growing interest in myth-making and a new awareness of its importance. Even fairy tales are no longer regarded as nonsensical inventions written to amuse children, but as poetic creations that can reveal as much about the human psyche or the collective subconscious as a scientific study. In fact, myths are now the object of scientific study.

So it may well be that when a man today says "I suppose that Christ is really a kind of myth," he is not necessarily saying that what the church teaches that Christ is just a lot of pious fibs invented to provide false comfort for deluded worshipers. That kind of accusation would now be heard only in old-fashioned Marxist circles. Something much more subtle but perhaps even more destructive of Christian faith is usually meant. What they are saying is that the story of the Son of God becoming man, of his expiatory death and of his Resurrection is simply a variant of similar stories told about legendary figures in ancient Egypt, India, or other parts of the world. The Christmas story then becomes a myth expressing the idea of man's kinship with God; the Calvary story a myth expressing man's experience of tragedy; and the Easter story a myth expressing man's unconquerable hope.

When I say that this way of thinking is destructive of the Christian faith, I don't mean that there's something wicked about accepting Christian symbols and doctrines as poetic expressions of some of the deepest desires and emotions of the human heart. That the image of the Holy Child should express our delight in purity and innocence, that the star and the stories of the Savior's birth should renew our hopes for the human race, that angelic choirs should be an echo of mankind's longing for peace and goodwill—all this is surely a bonus for us in our secularized society. And who can deny that some element of myth in the deep sense of the word comes into all live religion?

But one thing has to be said loud and clear. Christianity came into being, and Christianity still continues to be alive because of something that really happened in this world we live in. Jesus Christ is not a myth but a real Person who was born about two thousand years ago as you and I were born, who lived and thought and talked and walked among the men of his day and died a cruelly real death. His first followers were not attracted to a story or an idea or a myth, but to a Person with

## I Suppose Christ Is Really a Kind of Myth

whom they had lived and worked. The church came into being, not as a society devoted in the first place to propagating certain ideas, but to announcing that something had happened in human history, something unique and almost unbelievable. In the first Christian sermon ever preached Peter didn't talk about an abstract hope and an ideal of Resurrection. He said: "This Jesus hath God raised up, whereof we are all witnesses." "This Jesus"—he was referring to someone his hearers knew. And he was prepared to say that he and his friends were witnesses of the Resurrection as a fact.

In the Apostles' Creed, which is very old and yet still accepted by all the great branches of the church today as expressing the content of the faith, we hear a drumbeat of factual statements—conceived, born, suffered, was crucified, dead, buried, rose again. This is a way of saying: "It happened; we believe in a real Person to whom these things happened." Some people would rather have a document that simply asserted principles and aspirations. But the church, I think, wisely keeps this assertion of the facts. For Christianity is an historic religion. It would never have appeared unless at a certain place and a certain time Christ really lived, really died, and really rose from the dead.

When people draw simple parallels between the Gospel stories and other tales of divine beings who died and rose again, they forget that no one nor-

OVERHEARD

mally claimed that these pagan myths referred to real historical characters. Prometheus, Hercules, Isis, and Osiris, or any other figure of classical mythology was not considered part of our human history. Their whole existence was in the world of myth. But the Gospels come to us with the story of a real human being and give us the names of his friends and of the various rulers with whom he had to deal. And the early Christians put the name of Pontius Pilate in the creed precisely because they wanted it known that they were talking of historical, datable events and not fantasies from a world of myth.

Of course there have been attempts to prove that Christ never existed but was the product of the imagination of an excitable sect in the early days of the Roman Empire. Even if we could suppose a group of Palestinian workingmen skillful enough to compose a story that has been accepted as fact by millions for two thousand years, a glance at the Gospels themselves should dispel any idea that this Christ could have been the creation of a committee of enthusiasts. They are too untidy for one thing. A fictional work would have been much neater. And they are full of unnecessary factual detail for anyone looking for a simple myth. They read like eyewitness accounts that converged on certain facts in spite of differences of outlook and detail—because that is what they are. In fact, there are very few scholars, whether Christian or not, who today would

## I Suppose Christ Is Really a Kind of Myth

uphold the theory that Christ is only a myth. Whatever else we believe about him, the historian would say, he is as real a character in human history as Julius Caesar or Abraham Lincoln.

Now suppose that the person we overhear saying that Christ is probably a kind of myth should be convinced that this is a shallow judgment and that he really did live, teach, heal, and die here on this earth, might he not want then to say "So what?" What difference does it make whether I believe that these things happened or not? Are the ideals of Jesus not just as valid whether or not he really lived, whether or not all these happened to him?

This is a fair question. We still believe that it's a good thing to tell the truth whether or not we believe the story about young George Washington and his father's cherry tree. Dutch people still believe in courage whether or not they believe in the story about the little boy with his finger in the hole in the dike. Scottish people still believe in patience whether or not they believe the story about Robert the Bruce watching a spider building up the web that had been broken. So why should we not go on believing in Christianity whether or not we accept the stories in the Gospels?

This is a question on which volumes have been written, but I want to spare you elaborate arguments. The simplest way to reply to this popular suggestion is to say that the Christian faith means a deeply personal commitment to Jesus Christ himself and not just to his ideas and ideals. Christians know him as One who does something for them because of who he is and what he did and what was done to him long ago. St. Paul, who knew how to talk at length about Christian doctrines, once summed the matter up by saying "To me to live is Christ." On another occasion he wrote of the one thing that mattered to him, "that I may know him, and the power of his Resurrection, and the fellowship of his suffering." You don't *know* a mythological figure like this, and you can't experience a real power in communion with him. Just as the greatest influence in our lives has usually been exerted by a person, father, mother, friend, and not by an abstract idea, so the influence of God himself according to the Gospel comes through a real Person and not a doctrine.

I would invite anyone who has been tempted to be satisfied with the ideas of Christianity while rejecting most of the story to have another look at the record. "Come and behold him!" as the carol says. Let him rise from the Gospel pages in all his humanity before you worry about what we call his divinity. Listen to him and see if there is not something more here than just a set of moral precepts. Note how he speaks so often about his coming as if his appearance on earth was decisive for people like you and me. "I am come that they might have life,

## I Suppose Christ Is Really a Kind of Myth

and that they might have it more abundantly." "The Son of Man is come to seek and to save that which was lost." "The Son of Man came not to be ministered unto, but to minister, and to give his life a ransom for many." It was to him that men were drawn, and they found in him something more than a teacher, something more than a leader.

We realize that we should never have heard of this Jesus unless the apostles had preserved these words. And when we ask why they did we find it was not just to commemorate the thoughts and deeds of one who had died. It was to introduce us to One whom they knew to be still alive. If they did not believe in the Resurrection none of them would have written a line about Christ, and there would have been no church.

I am thinking now about some of the remarkable Christians of our own day—Schweitzer, Karl Barth, Bonhoeffer, Pope John, Teilhard de Chardin, and others who have made their mark on the life and thought of the modern world. These have been men of strikingly different personality and temperament, yet I can't think of one who was motivated by a devotion simply to the *ideas* of Christianity, or who would have been satisfied with this notion of a glorious myth. They have all been men who came under the spell of Christ as a Person, and their works reflect in varied ways their communion with him. And when we think of others who have been won to the faith from a position of agnosticism—G. K. Chesterton, C. S. Lewis, C. E. M. Joad, Lin Yutang, Malcolm Muggeridge—in every case it was the reality of Christ, himself, and not just the ideas for which he stood that made them Christian. I cannot think of a single example in our times of a man or woman converted to the faith by anything less than the full-orbed presentation of Christ such as that enshrined in the Apostles' Creed.

Muggeridge, for instance, in his *Jesus Rediscovered*, has this to say: "It was while I was in the Holy Land for the purpose of making three BBC television programs on the New Testament that a curious, almost magical, certainty seized me about Jesus' birth, ministry, and Crucifixion. I became aware that there really had been a man, Jesus, who was also God—I was conscious of his presence. He really had spoken these sublime words—I heard them. He really had died on a Cross and risen from the dead. Otherwise, how was it possible for me to meet him, as I did—in the desert wrestling with the Devil, on that hillside preaching of how the meek inherit the earth and the pure of heart see God, falling in step along the road to Emmaus. As I tried to explain in my commentary the words Jesus spoke are living words, as relevant today as when they were first spoken; the light he shone continues to shine as brightly as ever. Thus he is alive, as for instance Socrates—who also chose to lay down his

## I Suppose Christ Is Really a Kind of Myth

life for truth's sake—isn't. . . . the Resurrection is historical; Jesus is alive and very truth. The Cross is where history and life, legend and reality, time and eternity, intersect. There, Jesus is nailed for ever to show us how God could become a man and a man become God."

I believe there are many who in their own way could make this rediscovery of Jesus, and would find that, far from being "a kind of myth" he is still a living presence and a power.

# I Live a Pretty Decent Life: What More Do I Need?

When I was a boy in Scotland, New Year's Eve was a big occasion. For various reasons it loomed even larger in our lives than Christmas. The churches had what we called Watch Night services; there were parties all over the place, and after midnight had struck and "Auld Lang Syne" had been sung, the streets were full of people going the rounds of each other's homes. This was called "first footing" —since the person who first put his foot over your doorstep in the New Year was supposed to bring good luck and a little present.

In the High Street of Edinburgh the celebrations were, and still are, particularly lively. But what struck me as a boy was the curious contrast of St. Giles and what was happening outside. Inside, a large congregation sang the psalms and hymns, listened to a solemn sermon, and then remained in quiet prayer under the old arches and ancient battle flags until the great bell of the church tolled out the news of midnight and the beginning of another year. Outside was a scene of wild carnival with surging crowds linking arms and singing, shouting, blow-

## I Live a Pretty Decent Life: What More Do I Need?

ing hooters, and consuming quantities of whisky. I'm not saying that the people inside the church were entirely divorced from the merriment. Most of them emerged to share it. But I couldn't help noticing the difference between the solemn religious stocktaking that went on in church and the reckless, happy-go-lucky atmosphere outside.

Now I suppose this year in America there will be some people in church on New Year's Eve and that there will be others who make a point of prayer and meditation as the year draws to its close. But the large majority will slide into the New Year on a wave of secular cordiality, wishing one another good luck and hoping for better days ahead. I don't imagine they would want a preacher to intrude with a summons to cut out the frivolity and think of their immortal souls and the inevitable finale to which each New Year is hurrying us on.

I've no desire to break up anyone's New Year party with a blistering sermon or to condemn the jovial custom of greeting the New Year with a song and a toast, but I am curious about the tendency to think of religion as an intrusion on such occasions. It's almost as if the public has come to think of worship and prayer as a kind of extra, very suitable at weddings and funerals, but only important to a limited number of people on other occasions. Everyone is very happy that those who want to can exercise their constitutional right to practice their re-

**OVERHEARD**

ligion, but many feel happiest with their own right to be left alone and not troubled with religious questions, either on New Year's Eve or any other time.

What I have in mind is the attitude expressed by a remark you can overhear whenever the suggestion is made that religion has something to offer to modern man or when perhaps he is invited to come to church: "I live a pretty decent life; what more do I want?" Behind this lies the notion that religion is indeed a kind of extra, an extra that happens to appeal to a certain kind of person but which is quite unnecessary for the average, good-living citizen. Sometimes a well-meaning churchman who gets this answer to his approach is baffled as to how to reply. For indeed the person he is speaking to may be a most attractive fellow, possibly far more attractive than some church members that he knows. And what he says seems to make sense. Here is a law-abiding, conscientious, generous, good-hearted soul always ready to give a helping hand. What more could religion give him, except perhaps a kind of mystical experience that he probably doesn't want?

Before I attempt an answer I want to make it clear that I am not assuming that this nonreligious man has no serious thoughts about the purpose of his life or the reality of a God. It may well be that at times, toward the end of a year perhaps, he does some reckoning about the way his life is going, the sort of accounting that goes far beyond dollars and

## I Live a Pretty Decent Life: What More Do I Need?

cents. He has his moments when something he can only call God comes into the picture. But he just doesn't see the need to make a fuss about it, to spend any time worrying about doctrines that seem impossibly remote from his daily concerns, to expose himself to all the demands that churches seem to make on their members. "If I live by my own conscience," he says, "that's good enough; those who like the religious trimmings can have them."

Well, let's start with this business of conscience and see where it takes us. By our conscience we mean that inner voice that tells us we have or have not lived up to what we know to be right. The man who says "I live a pretty decent life" means that, apart from a few slips, his conscience tells him that he's doing all right. This at once raises the question of what our conscience is telling us, whether or not it is reliable, and if it is not possible for a conscience to become more or less sensitive as the years pass. If we think about it seriously it will be apparent that a conscience is not something like a moral alarm clock that is set to go off in everyone's inside at exactly the same time. When a man says he obeys his conscience we may want to examine the kind of conscience he has. Some of the most ghastly crimes in history have been committed by conscientious men. How do you react for instance when a soldier is asked on television what he felt like when shooting down women and children, and he replies that he

135

OVERHEARD

felt it was all right because his superior ordered him to do it? Was there nothing wrong with that kind of conscience?

No, conscience is not something automatic and universal in its judgments. It is not an instinct on which we can rely to deliver an infallible ruling. Every one of us has developed a conscience according to the moral teachings to which we have been exposed. As each year passes we become either more ethically sensitive or less. To some extent it depends on the company we keep. A kid whose conscience at home tells him it's wrong to take drugs may very quickly find himself in an environment of his peers where conscience seems no longer to say the same thing. If a man spends long enough in a business where ethical corners are regularly cut, he may soon find that his former standards of honesty no longer speak to his conscience. Conversely, we have all known how the friendship of a really good man or woman or the love of a wonderful parent or spouse can raise our moral sights and make our conscience a more sensitive instrument in our daily life.

So when we overhear "I live a pretty decent life," we can't help wondering a little about the standard of measurement. Without querying the integrity of the man who says this I would want to push a little farther into this matter of the decent life. On analysis I believe that by a "decent life" most people mean one that approximates to the standards of the

## I Live a Pretty Decent Life: What More Do I Need?

civilization we have inherited. Ethically that means the moral ideals we get from the Bible. Now these moral ideals came to us in and with the religion of the Bible, and as I have said before, it is very doubtful if they can be maintained indefinitely without the support of that religion. Therefore, I would want to ask the man who claims to live by these standards and to have no need of the religion if he is confident that the next generation is going to inherit them automatically. I rather suspect that he is not, for quite often the man who says he has no need for religion does try to expose his children to the moral influence of the church. The "decent life" is not so divorced from its religious origins as many seem to think.

Then there is this question about educating our conscience and the company we keep. How do we know whether our ideas about what constitutes a decent life are not slipping a bit as the years go on? Most of us need some sort of check; otherwise it is very easy to have our conscience gradually taken over by popular opinion or the mood of the day. I find a lot of older people today alarmed by the shifting standards of the younger generation. But if the so-called "decent life" is based on no more than the habits of our contemporaries then the young may be quite right to challenge them in the name of the habits of *their* contemporaries. What is surely needed is a new recognition that there is a moral demand on

OVERHEARD

us that is much more stringent than any temporary way of life, a demand that has its roots in something deeper than popular mores. It is to this inner Voice that every generation has to respond, each in its own way. Our consciences have to be educated by being exposed to the constant appeal of the God who made us and knows what he would have us to be.

This is the "something more" that true religion provides. We are asked to keep company with the very highest we can know and to let our consciences be educated by nothing less than the perfect will of God for us. To put it in more concrete terms, I can keep my ideas of the "decent life" alive and growing only as I keep company with God. That's the "something more" that we need.

And how does this work out in a living religion? I can only now talk about Christianity since that is the faith to which I am committed and the religion of which I have some experience. The Christian knows that there is a level of life revealed in Jesus which makes it impossible for him ever to be satisfied with the moral plateau he may have reached. He respects the moral code in which he has been raised and the standards of the decent people around him, but he keeps hearing the voice that says "What do ye more?" To keep company with Christ is to have one's conscience continually renewed and sensitized. It is, of course, possible for our prayers or church attendance to be merely routine and formal, and

## I LIVE A PRETTY DECENT LIFE: WHAT MORE DO I NEED?

no one would dare to claim that Christians are always notably more morally sensitive than others. But what a glorious opportunity we have! To be reminded of the law of God, to be challenged by the life of Christ, to be stimulated by the presence of the living Spirit—is this not something more that is infinitely worthwhile?

But I would say that there is something even more needed than this constant check upon our conscience and concept of the "decent life." The kind of religion you find in the New Testament overthrows this whole idea of justifying ourselves with words like "I live a pretty decent life." Religious people are often accused of being smug and self-satisfied, but real Christianity should have exactly the opposite effect. Every word and story of Christ and the apostles seems designed to demonstrate that none of us has, as it were, a moral leg to stand on in the presence of our God. The Sermon on the Mount, which some are not afraid to tell you is "all the religion they want," is a devastating document. Read it again, and I'm sure you'll not end up saying "That's the kind of life I lead; so I don't need any of the proffered resources of religion." The people that Christ lamented most were not the rogues and the profligate but the proud and the self-satisfied. The man who said "God, be merciful to me a sinner" was, he said, "justified" because he didn't try to justify himself. That was what the other did who recounted his "decent life" and thanked God he was not like other men. I don't know any way of breaking out of our self-justification more powerful than this—to let Christ show us that we have nothing to boast about before other men, least of all in his presence.

Then I can't help wondering about the assumption that we can live up to our best ideals without any dynamic from beyond ourselves. The briefest prayer that I have heard recently went like this: "Almighty and everlasting God . . . help!" Isn't that how most of us really feel? "Almighty and everlasting God . . ."—the words remind us of someone we have heard of ever since we were small. We repeat them, and then all we find we want to say is "Help!" Not a bad prayer, for it expresses exactly what we need. If you have ever struggled with a strong temptation, if you have ever despaired of being the kind of person you really want to be, if you have ever faced a situation that was quite beyond your powers to cope with, if you have ever reached the blank spot where all the usual lights go out, then you know what it means to utter this simple cry for help.

It is here, but not only here, that real religion speaks. I'm not advocating religion as a last resort, for unless we have some training in it the desperate cry for help may have little reality in it. God should be not the last but the first resort, which means that we allow his Spirit to work in us day by day.

I Live a Pretty Decent Life: What More Do I Need?

His grace is not an emergency exit when the house is on fire. It is the light by which we seek to live that "decent life" in all its rooms day by day. And the Christ who shows us how far short we have all come is the same Christ who accepts us as we are and comes to live with us with all his transforming power.

In my consideration of these various remarks that one overhears today about religion, I have tried to understand and sympathize with what is being expressed. I also understand the person who finds conventional religion an unnecessary extra and feels he can do without it. But I can't help passing on my conviction that true religion such as a living contact with Jesus Christ gives a meaning and a deep joy that nothing else can provide. What I want above all to pass on is not my own outlook on life or my thoughts on current points of view but the Gospel of Christ—the Good News that God is, that God cares, that he cares so much that he gave his Son to experience our life, our loneliness, and our death, and has invited us all to find the new, the eternal life in him. It is he who awaits your response.